NEWS TO ME
GOSPEL STORIES
FOR THE REAL WORLD

Lawrence Wood

Westminster John Knox Press
LOUISVILLE • LONDON

Block quotations of scripture, unless otherwise indicated, are from the New Revised Standard Version of the Bible, copyright © 1989 by the Division of Christian Education of the National Council of the Churches of Christ in the U.S.A., and used by permission. Scripture quotations throughout the text are either NRSV or the author's paraphrases.

Scripture quotations marked NIV are from *The Holy Bible, New International Version.* Copyright © 1973, 1978, 1984 International Bible Society. Used by permission of Zondervan Bible Publishers.

Scripture quotations marked RSV are from the Revised Standard Version of the Bible, copyright © 1946, 1952, 1971, and 1973 by the Division of Christian Education of the National Council of the Churches of Christ in the U.S.A., and are used by permission.

Some portions of these chapters originally appeared in *The Christian Century:* "Taste Test" by Larry Wood. Copyright © 2002 by the *Christian Century.* Reprinted by permission from the October 23, 2002, issue of the *Christian Century.* "Labors of Love" by Larry Wood. Copyright © 2003 by the *Christian Century.* Reprinted by permission from the May 17, 2003, issue of the *Christian Century.* "Everything Must Go" (originally published as "A Lot of Junk") by Larry Wood. Copyright © 2004 by the *Christian Century.* Reprinted by permission from the July 27, 2004, issue of the *Christian Century.* "Otherwise," copyright 2005 by the Estate of Jane Kenyon. Reprinted from *Collected Poems* with the permission of Graywolf Press, Saint Paul, Minnesota.

Book design by Sharon Adams
Cover design by Mark Abrams
Cover photograph: Getty Images/Steve Bloom

First edition
Published by Westminster John Knox Press
Louisville, Kentucky

This book is printed on acid-free paper that meets the American National Standards Institute Z39.48 standard. ∞

PRINTED IN THE UNITED STATES OF AMERICA

08 09 10 11 12 13 14 15 16 17 — 10 9 8 7 6 5 4 3 2 1

Library of Congress Cataloging-in-Publication Data

Wood, Lawrence.
    News to me : gospel stories for the real world / Lawrence Wood. — 1st ed.
        p. cm.
    Includes bibliographical references.
    ISBN 978-0-664-23226-9 (alk. paper)
    1. Christian life. I. Title.

BV4501.3.W653 2008
242—dc22

                                                                2007032143

This book is for
Rexene and Hannah

Contents

vi   Contents

Overture

When I was fourteen years old, I got a job writing for my hometown's evening newspaper, the *Evansville Press.* (The evening paper doesn't exist any longer. One stunning day, the Scripps-Howard chain, which owned the *Press,* bought its morning competitor and cleared house, firing most of the best people from the better paper and replacing them with loyalists from the *Press.* The city's most beloved columnist had a heart attack during the announcement and died at his desk.) I took my start in the promising world of journalism and happily wrote a weekly column for next to nothing.

Within a few years I was making minimum wage covering stories all over town. (The road I traveled most frequently doesn't exist any longer; it was taken up for an elevated expressway.) Some of my assignments were quite memorable, and I have good memories of hanging out afternoons in the press box of the thoroughbred racetrack, although usually I was assigned tasks like the agate page, that is, the small type of box scores.

Three paces away from my desk was a small room called the morgue, where thousands of clippings had been filed by author and subject. For a while it pleased me to pad my own file at the morgue, but at last I had to admit that the evanescent nature of journalism didn't satisfy my ambition. I aspired to write fiction, lasting fiction, something truly brilliant and permanent. (It didn't occur to me that even fine books by famous authors didn't last—that those books

1

are sold at garage sales, then cut close to the spine to fit on short shelves in decorative faux libraries.)

It turned out that that weekly column had been good practice for preaching, but I never lost the desire to write something that would last. I wondered how veteran preachers who really worked at their craft could just let their work disappear into the ether. When I asked the painstaking Emery Percell if he had thought of publishing his sermons, he sadly shook his head and said:

"A good sermon is like a newspaper. It tells you the news for today, if it is any good, and then yellows with age."

—⁂—

Somewhere in ancient North Africa, a novice writer took in his hand a brush made of boar's hair, dipped it in ink made of berries, and wrote on a scroll made of papyrus leaves. Spread before him were earlier accounts of the life he was going to write. We have some of those documents; others we can only imagine. The light in which he wrote may have been bad—maybe an oil lamp. This writer had no thought for people a thousand or two thousand years ahead. So far as he knew, the world might evaporate like dew on the morning grass in his own generation. Yet something motivated him to put these stories to paper. He was writing the gospel of John.

The good news is indeed old, and strange, and to some not quite credible. And it is still news. News to me, too. It comes to us personally—delivered, some fine day, to our doorstep, apparently by accident, so perhaps we may decide to subscribe to it.

Today I'm sitting with a man, not yet old, who has been told he will die soon of cancer. His face is jaundiced and peaceful. Eight years ago he drank heavily; no one ever expected him to die of liver *cancer;* yet he hasn't touched a drop in all these years and has quietly come to a life of faith. Some of his kids have too, some have not.

He is lying on a sofa in a trailer home, all kinds of thoughts surely going through his mind, which doesn't work quite so well as before, although his eyes don't tell much of what he's thinking. All his wife's thoughts are written on her face: they just found out today. God help us in such a moment. We think we have to find the right words, but really it's okay to say anything, even something stupid—we all just need to hear each others' voices.

"So are you getting any sleep these days?"

"No, what I really want to do is stay awake."

He's scared, she's scared, I'm scared, but there's this faith among us spoken and unspoken as long as we're together. Our relationship is one of faith that this isn't the end. The kids are going to need this. We talk about one of them, a son who doesn't get home often and seems pretty worried over the telephone. We talk about practical matters like insurance, and her time off work, and whether they'd like church folks to help them lay up some meals. We talk about hospice, which will be coming in a few days, and the concern of their friends.

As we wait for a daughter to arrive, I offer a prayer; we all join hands—his is surprisingly dry and warm. Wind rattles the little trailer. I am embarrassed that my words have even a trace of an easy practiced rhythm inadequate to the moment. Thank God his wife adds her prayer, which manages simultaneously to quote the gospel and speak for her husband, too.

Against the evidence, I still believe, believe even more strongly, that what we do and say has lasting significance. Even if the sun burns out and all human striving ceases to make a sound in the cosmos, what we have done will matter. As long as we have each other, it matters very much.

My friend knows that his faith will survive him. And if most writing involves the hope for fame, preaching is a more modest hope, no, a certainty, that the message will outlive the teller.

—⚘—

We have nothing that Jesus wrote: only a tantalizing image of him writing. A woman had been caught in the act of adultery and dragged before a crowd of men ready to kill her for the crime. As the crowd seethed around her, Jesus, who was already known to consort with prostitutes, knelt and wrote with his finger in the sand.

The crowd hushed, waiting for this literate man to quote the scripture that would condemn her. Instead, he said, "Let any who is without sin cast the first stone." Scandalously, he even told her, "Neither do I condemn you," which some people might take as an admission of his own sin.

Frankly it's amazing that this appears in John's gospel. The author had so much to tell about Jesus that "if everything he did were written down, I suppose the world itself could not contain the books that would be written." Some of the tales were just strange, such as how the boy Jesus had fashioned a living bird from clay or struck playmates dead. Other materials were truly interesting but of uncertain provenance, or turned out to be doublets of earlier stories. Earlier writers had already given the who, what, where, when. This writer wanted to convey the mystery of being in the presence of one who called the Creator his Father.

There was so much to tell and there were so many things to leave out. So when our novice writer came to a scandalous story that didn't necessarily do Jesus a lot of credit, his pen must have hesitated.

Should he leave this one out? (Maybe for a while he did. The earliest manuscripts of his gospel do not have it.) But other thoughts came to him, too. Perhaps, before he had come to this ascetic community in northern Africa where fellow believers dressed in white robes, he had taken love from equally careless women and had lived the life of a libertine. It was not the proudest chapter of his life.

There in the dark, as a dog barked in the street, he thought about it.

The things we would rather not remember, the things that embarrass us in ourselves, our heroes, even in Jesus, may be in the end the most important of all. The most important story about my friend is how he stopped drinking and took up a new, fragile life in Christ. It redeemed countless sins that weighed more heavily on him, perhaps, than on anyone else. It gave an entirely different cast to the second part of his life. That's primarily what his kids want to say, through their many anecdotes.

This may be why the writer of the gospel of John plunged ahead and started a new paragraph. Indeed, the whole story is about a new paragraph. *Neither do I condemn you. Go and sin no more.* It is the gospel in indelible sand—how Jesus wrote with his finger on the ground.

I have often wondered about that haunting detail. What did he write? Did it have anything to do with the woman whose life seemed to be at the very end? What mark did he make?

For the sake of my friend, I would like to imagine that he made this mark:

¶

New paragraph.

Somewhere even today, in a place where the light is bad, someone is trying to find just the right words for a story that will be read only by God. Meanwhile, with just one mark, Jesus would have written a gospel.

Who

Jordan Stones

They are there to this day.
Joshua 4:9

*F*ind your way back, if you can, across the wide waters, and then to your earliest memory. Pick up something solid if it helps. Strangers, your relatives, wait on the other side, with beliefs of their own but without any of the everyday miracles you take for granted.

The Israelites stood on the west side of the Jordan. In crossing it they had experienced the power of God, and no one objected when Joshua said they should mark the spot with twelve stones, one for each tribe. The stones, as large as sheep, were slippery and heavy, and the strong men who carried them had to work fast because the waters might close in on them at any moment. A day before, the Jordan had been in full flood with melted snow; now this part of the riverbed had gone strangely, miraculously dry.

On Joshua's instructions, men brought those twelve stones to the shore and arranged them in a circle. To put a stone where it has not been before is to indulge a little in God's prerogative. Who has not felt a little guilty at throwing a stone back into the ocean? And yet this time it seemed so obviously right, a humble testament to what God alone could do, God's amazing prerogative to pick up and put the Hebrews here. It was the very land that God had shown their ancestors. They named the place Gilgal, which is Hebrew for circle—and how appropriate that was, for they had come full circle. They had been this way before, as they would again.

But the stones have not stayed there; no one has seen them for thousands of years. Nor has anyone seen twelve others that Joshua himself arranged in the riverbed where the priests of the twelve tribes had stood. Why he did this we can only guess, for as soon as the waters came back the stones must have disappeared from view, unless the very idea of them was supposed to lead us back to our forebears. If we put our feet in the river, the mud sucks at our soles. Maybe the hoary old metaphor, that time is a river, means that in certain timeless moments we can pass right across its dry bed to our own ancestors. So we may not be a long ways downriver from them, but only across the river.

—⟶⟶⟶—

Why should we go back there? That is the question any time we pick up the Bible.

It comes from a long time ago when people saw different events with different eyes and used a language, now dead in every way, to describe those dead conditions. All that we know of these people must be imagined from shards of pottery, scraps of scrolls; their very lives are hieroglyphics. Why should we even bother with those ghosts? To go back there may be like journeying into realms of the dead, where the air is spent and stale, and the river we must cross might not be the Jordan but the Styx.

But then again—we might be the ones who are dead, wandering about as if in sleep, while those supposed ancients are actually more awake to the world, nearer its source, more alive.

On this side of the river, life is getting complicated. I can sit all day staring at a computer screen and then take a cell phone with me elsewhere, so work is always at hand, blinking and bleeping. Some people actually walk down the street talking into a headset— such as this stunning woman in an Ann Taylor dress with a long-shoreman's mouth, who seems not quite sane, even if someone really is listening to her. "I can't believe the flipping luck," she cries into her headset. "I left a cup of yogurt on my laptop, and the damn thing *melted!*" Life is so complicated that preachers feel a need to simplify the Bible vastly and make it contemporary, offering a church with no robes, no creeds, no candles, no ceremony, praise music that sounds like pop music, and elaborately choreographed messages like business seminars.

Sooner or later, though, we have to reckon with the Bible in all its ancient strangeness. I don't know anyone who drives flocks of sheep across a wilderness. Most people today don't set great store by their dreams or visions. And we certainly don't mark rivers we have crossed with stones. The only place to find comparable strangeness today is in a traditional church. An old congregation with its creaking pews, sooty stained glass, hymns from another generation, acolytes, vestments, and paraments, doesn't seem part of modern life. And because it doesn't cater to me, any more than the scripture does, it *is* about me, rather than some marketer's idea of me. It is a little strip of timelessness where the ground is soft, dirty, and damp.

I am pretty sure that faith is closely related to memory. Indeed, one of the benefits of faith is meeting our ancestors as real men and women, as flesh-and-blood creatures. We start to wonder what they ate, what made them laugh, what music they danced to, how water tasted to them. The Bible is full of these Jordan stones.

—⟋⟍—

In September of 1845, just after putting up the late summer hay, a sixty-four-year-old carpenter named Elias and his wife Susanna loaded a wagon with items they couldn't depend on finding elsewhere, left their home in New York State, and set out westward, hoping to finish their journey before snow fell.

Like many others of his generation, he had been restless. His father had left the seacoast for the Berkshire Mountains of western Massachusetts, beautiful country with plenty of hardwood and a valley for dairy farming. But by the time Elias was grown, adventurous folk were heading south through the mountains in search of cheaper, less crowded land. Elias followed them down the Appalachians, over to Kentucky and Indiana, seeing his first and second wives through childbirth in inhospitable places before settling at last in the Genesee, a heavily forested, lightly settled hill region of western New York State.

By then his eldest sons were itching to make their marks in the wilderness of Michigan. It sounded like a terrible idea—everyone knew that the Lower Peninsula was a swamp fit only for timber wolves and disease. As it turned out, the boys chose some of the rockiest, least productive land anywhere. They would be pulling up stones from their plows for years. But they worked hard to bring it under cultivation, and ten years later they called for their aged father, who still had young children at home.

This would be his last journey. At sixty-four, with his third wife ailing, Elias knew that his youngest children needed extended family.

Susanna shivered against his shoulder as he shook the reins and the wagon lurched forward. A little girl, pressed against her, could not keep her warm. They rode to Buffalo, then boarded a steamship for Detroit. The waves were rough that time of year; to anyone unfamiliar with such vast waters, Lake Erie must have been eerie—almost Biblical.

—⟪⟫—

The very name Jordan, in Hebrew, means Descender. The name indicates that the river comes from a great height, fed by snow from the mountains. It also stands for the people most associated with the river—that is, Abraham's descendants.

Abraham, you will remember, remained childless until very late in life. Today his descendants can scarcely be counted; in fact, when you consider those of us who have been adopted, it's the largest family in the world.

So the river and its name must have felt very significant to Joshua and the Israelites as they came to the east side of the Jordan. For forty years, they had gone the long way around the Sinai

Peninsula; then up from there, along the east side of the Dead Sea, almost completing the circle *(gilgal)* that Abraham had started.

What a heady homecoming! It must have been like journeying forward and backward in time.

And it would have become even eerier when God parted the waters of the Jordan, just as for an earlier generation he had parted the Red Sea. Now there are two ways of picturing this miracle redux. One is that the river simply dammed up. The other image is even stranger—that it continued to flow except for a dry path in the midst of flowing waters; a little strip of timelessness, a place where the Hebrews literally passed through history.

Abraham's descendants kept coming back to that spot, their history a series of echoes. The Hebrews would say that the great prophet Elijah also stopped the Jordan River with his mantle, and crossed from this life into the next; and on that spot his spiritual son, Elisha, picked up his mantle. John the Baptist called Jews to repentance in the sacred river, admonishing, "Do not say to yourselves, 'We have Abraham for our ancestor,' for I tell you, God is able to raise up children of Abraham from these very stones!" One young man entered the waters and heard, "This is my child, my beloved, with whom I am well-pleased."

You, too, may have been there a long time ago, a different era of your life. Now your feet are dry, but the soles of your shoes remember when you crossed the Jordan. Mud sucked at your feet, and throughout the crossing you hoped the waters would not pour back in. You remember how you came here, coming to terms with childlessness, still hoping for just one, hardly daring to hope for many children.

—∿—

Several years ago, my grandmother died and I was asked to conduct the burial at Lee Center, Michigan, where my father's family came from. I myself had not been there in years. Nothing had changed, except for a barn falling in.

Lee Center is little more than a crossroads, far from any town of

size. My great-great-grandfather Charles helped to build the old
Methodist church, a white frame, one-room meetinghouse full of
old photographs, such as one of my grandfather surrounded by his
Sunday school mates at the age of ten. Not far is an old family
home with a fieldstone "Michigan basement." My father spent
summers in these fields as a boy, picking up stones ahead of the
plow and tossing them into the stone boat.

Just a quarter mile behind the church was the Lee Center Cemetery. Rexene and I walked there along the shoulder of a country
road, our clasped hands warm and sweaty.

We had recently had our second miscarriage. Or maybe it was
our fifth—depending on what it had meant when her period came
very late. At any rate, it was becoming plain that we weren't going
to have kids of our own. Years of attempts, less and less romantic,
were sapping our marriage. She wanted so much to be a mother;
for all her other gifts, it was what she most wanted to do with her
life. I professed not to be so anxious for a child, but in reality, even
though there was no good reason for feeling this way, I feared dis-
appointing my father as I had when I became a pastor. The family
name would stop with me.

Rexene asked, "Now, who did Charles marry, again?" We had
spoken of some of these family names for a child.

She gave me a squeeze as we passed through the gates. It was a
little weedy and the air buzzed with the songs of insects. For such
a small place, there were more markers than we could take in very
easily. Many were bone-white and worn smooth by the wind, but
others were startlingly new and clear.

"Hmm," she said, seeing a stone where my grandmother's date
would be filled in.

We stumbled upon my great-grandfather Earl's stone, and then
the gravestone of his father, Charles, who had come from New
York State to Lee Center at the age of thirteen. When his family
had reached Detroit, they had traveled on plank roads until they
picked up the Michigan Central Railroad. The line, which followed
an old Indian trail, ended at Marshall. There they had hired a
wagon for his mother and sister; the men had walked the twenty
miles to Lee and built a cabin before snow fell.

So two other forebears had to be nearby. It took some doing, but we found their names on a stone in the southwest corner:

WOOD

Elias	Susanna
October 17, 1781	August 14, 1800
August 22, 1867	October 18, 1846

They had stood on this hill, they had walked through this grass. Susanna had made it to his birthday before she died. The stone noted, "First burial in Lee Center Cemetery."

All the years were as nothing for the brief moment in which the cares of these people, their clothing, their breathing, were as real as our own. They weren't just figures from stories. They were real people. They couldn't have foreseen us very clearly, just as we didn't know that scarcely a year later a child would come into our lives.

Their families had washed the bodies, dug the graves, dressed the dead in their best clothes, hired a preacher, and paid to have a stone cut so that someone years later, someone they couldn't even imagine, would come here and know who they were. Someday the engravings would vanish, the stones themselves would vanish altogether—but the family memories would not necessarily be lost. The stones were put here, and *they are there to this day.*

Although the stories remain, and Joshua and his people remain as alive as ever in the pages of the Bible, people have searched without success for those stones in the Jordan. I would like to think that they are still there. Rounded somewhat by the waters of three thousand years, they may wait for our feet to make the crossing. Like stones in the water, memory grows smooth and rounded, and sooner or later we come full circle.

Drop-Dead Gorgeous

"*I*t's true. I swear it's true," Bill says.

"The president of France," I say.

"In 1899 the president of France died of pleasure, and his mistress had to be . . . pulled from him. Can you believe it?" He takes a drink and says, "I think one of the Rockefellers died the same way."

We are at a wedding with lots of scenery. Today the male gaze is welcome. Every male indulges, even the oldest and youngest. You can see wonder in the eyes of a little boy, all of eight years old, amid a forest of bare, scented legs.

Here is a young gazelle who aspires to a beauty myth, that persistent literary figure the *femme fatale,* who supposedly is so pretty that she can literally stop your heart. Bill is determined to get as close as possible.

She is sipping champagne, one elbow cupped by the other hand, looking around at the bridesmaids. Dressed in white, but much more simply than the bride, she could be drawn from your imagination, which in fact she is.

Bill asks, "Have you tried the crab puffs?"

"I don't eat crab. Shellfish," she says. "But yes, they were delicious. Thanks for ruining them for me."

"Don't mention it," he says. "I could also tell you the maid of honor has eaten two plates of shrimp. I think it's her payment for the dress."

"I don't think the girls look that bad," she says. "Do you?" And she turns to show her classic profile, the clean line of her chin, the whorls of her ears.

Not often at a loss for words, Bill almost suffers a failure of nerve. Fortunately she dispenses justifying grace—if not the sanctifying kind that could actually improve him—as she hands him a plastic cup of champagne.

"They say you can taste what's in the soil . . . cinnamon, oak, apple," he ventures, swirling the champagne and holding it to his nose. "Now, besides the box this came in, I think you can taste . . . Pachelbel. Cuisinart. K-Mart. It has a good nose, which must be the groom's father's. And a little bouquet carried by a bridesmaid. Most of all, though," he says, "most of all, I can taste the possibility of lovely company, something cool, brisk, and intoxicating, and I could stand here with you all day hoping to drink my fill."

"Oh, you're full of it, all right," she laughs with an easy toss of her pale mane and gallops off.

Defeated but delighted, Bill smiles as if to say: there is a God.

A woman's beauty is a form of divinity—which is to say it enters the realm of myth. It gives delight, but also proves impossible to live up to, especially for women. Who can be a goddess? Supposing one could "thick men's blood with cold," is that any way to live? And don't goddesses have tragic ends when they are changed into something else? Even for *la belle dame sans merci,* there is no *merci.*

It should be enough just to be the woman God created, with mottled skin and reddish hair that never lies flat. Such a natural woman is, let's face it, more than enough to show the hand of God.

But the church doesn't tell her that. It doesn't mention beauty at all. Instead of making every woman feel that she is a miracle, the church leaves the celebration of beauty to the business world, which tells her she must spend, sweat, and starve herself toward some glossy ideal.

No, the church celebrates the Virgin Mary, a woman idealized in a completely different, sexless direction. It misses the connection between an incarnational God and sensual pleasure.

So very naturally, but without any help from the church, ordinary people become theologians of beauty. We celebrate, honor, and question beautiful people and works of art. We delight in music and movies, in gardens, in athletics performed with grace, in dance, in faces. We compare beautiful things passionately, and our questions about them are ultimately theological: *Where did this come from? What does it mean? Is it any good?* It's not hard for us to connect sex, beauty, and our love of them to a Creator.

"Every experience of beauty points to infinity," said a Swiss priest, Hans Urs von Balthasar. Certain pleasures did that for him intensely: Mozart, for example. At the end of a long day, he would sit down at the piano and play *Don Giovanni* from memory. (He knew Mozart's music so well that eventually he gave away his phonographs.) Perhaps no one in the last century thought more deeply about the relationship between aesthetics and God. Some officials in the Catholic Church welcomed this exploration, and some did not. For decades he maintained a close though chaste relationship with his muse, Adrienne von Speyr, even sharing a home with her, despite the rumors; and together they created hundreds of manuscripts. Though not conventionally beautiful, she undoubtedly became the great love of this priest's life. Balthasar often seemed a poet rather than a philosopher. Once he was so bored by a dry academic discussion that he left muttering, "All the eros has gone out of theology." The first volume of his massive *Explorations in Theology* is titled *The Word Made Flesh,* and it amounts to a sigh: there is a God.

—⋙—

Beauty is part of God's prodigality. God did not need to create a world quite this lovely; it could have been strictly utilitarian—

there is, after all, no need for the giraffe or hummingbird; no need for the song of a humpback whale, the drama of clouds, or the brilliant blue of lakes. And yet a world without such touches would be frightening. There are plenty of arguments for God, but perhaps the most persuasive is beauty.

Our response to beauty cannot easily be explained away. There are sensible explanations for how the zebra got its stripes, but none that explains my delight in a zebra. None that explains my attraction to inhospitable regions like Antarctica or a desert. And even if we have within us a bias for certain kinds of order, that doesn't explain why we reject some very orderly kinds of art as banal and instead admire the anarchic sort. Or find that banal as well.

Somehow the sight of dying leaves in brilliant color makes us feel more alive. We love it when a drama moves us to tears. Paint on a canvas does things to us beyond logic or reason. Moreover, we're not eager to learn much about the secret springs of this delight, because we want to preserve the mystery. My friend Bill, for example, is none too eager to lose a woman's mystery, because if he understood it in terms of pheromones from sweat glands and loving his mother, he would be sick to his stomach.

He is a theologian of beauty just as much as Balthasar, even though he has dribbled champagne on his tie. Listen to him go on about the women he regards as, well, goddesses.

"If you want to know who God is," he says by way of professional advice, "shut your books and use your eyes." Three bridesmaids kick off their shoes and rub their sore feet discreetly against their calves. One fishes in her purse for a roll of breath mints and passes them around. Bill is looking instead at the woman who spurned him when he says, "This is my church, let me tell you."

He does not seem to have noticed a perfectly fine young woman, very freckled, whose broad smile displays crowded teeth. She is totally without glamour and having the time of her life.

The figure in white has moved onto the parquet dance floor, surrounded by other young women at the height of their charms. Music seems to have been made for them. "That's who God is," Bill says. "God is beauty."

Well, maybe it is natural to look for God in beautiful things, but then again we may miss God sometimes because of that.

Nature has outdone itself here. This hotel was built on the site of an old quarry, and time has covered a multitude of sins done to the landscape. Here are hollyhocks and lilacs. In a generation, the ruins have grown grass and ivy, and polluted streams have been refreshed. Life has taken glorious hold of a homely place and reclaimed it.

And yet, as the beautiful young woman in white loiters by a neatly manicured trellis of roses, one can unaccountably remember some discordant verses:

> He grew up before him like a young plant,
>   and like a root out of dry ground;
> he had no form or majesty that we should look at him,
>   nothing in his appearance that we should desire him.
> He was despised and rejected by others;
>   a man of suffering and acquainted with infirmity;
> and as one from whom others hide their faces
>   he was despised, and we held him of no account.
>   (Isaiah 53:2–3)

Advice for Lonely Hearts

A hundred years ago, a newspaper newsroom was no place for a woman. Literally—at the New York *Evening Journal,* women were segregated in a room called the Hen Coop. As Marie Manning put it, "Forcing a man to work in the same room with us was the equivalent of sending a dog to the pound or standing a child in the corner."

In 1898, Miss Manning was twenty-six-years old. She longed to cover a murder trial or interview a politician, to cover real news.

One day her famous editor, Arthur Brisbane, walked into the Hen Coop with three letters the *Journal* had received from readers with personal problems, thinking one of the women would like to work these into a story. This wasn't real news, but it gave Marie an idea. What about a new feature, for people who needed advice? Plenty of people might confide to a sensitive stranger, just as they would to a priest. Brisbane thought it over. Well, maybe the young lady had something there. Of course Miss Manning couldn't write under her own name—that would be indiscreet. So she proposed the pen name Beatrice Fairfax, and a few days later the *Journal* advertised:

> Miss Beatrice Fairfax will advise you on the troubles of your heart. All young men and women have love affairs. At such times they need advice. Often it is impossible to obtain it from their families. Miss Fairfax has read and observed widely. She is young enough to sympathize with love's young dream. She will answer, to the best of her ability, all letters.[1]

The response astounded Brisbane. She received fourteen hundred letters a day; the post office refused to deliver such a volume, and the *Journal* had to hire two boys just to haul the mailbags.

Beatrice Fairfax, the first advice columnist, was a runaway success, largely because her advice was so good. Having survived an alcoholic father, she resisted the stereotypical wisdom that women should "suffer and be strong" and "hold fast to the male oak that supports the vine." And she brooked no foolishness:

Miss Beatrice Fairfax:

I have been keeping company with a young man for some time, and I love him. He seemed to love me in return, but he told me some time ago that he did not care to keep steady company, and he left me. . . . I asked him the last time if he thought we would ever go together again, and he said he could not tell, as at the present time he did not want any girl, but still he likes to go out with me. I keep company with a man who loves me, and I like him, but I do not love him as much as I do the other. . . . I would accept my first lover tomorrow. If I were to be married, and were at the altar with the second one, and could see the chance to marry the first, I would back out and return with my old love, if I knew he would be true to me.

Lida May

Lida May, you sentimental girls who lack pride and self-respect and call that lack "love" are rapidly destroying my sympathy with victims of the tender passion. Have you any ground for believing that a man who has played fast and loose with your feelings as your admirer would be a faithful or loving husband? Why don't you summon a little common sense to your aid? The man has insulted, rebuffed and wounded you. Could you possibly put yourself again in a position where he could again hurt you? A broken heart—I daresay you are suffering from that—is a trifling complaint compared to a bad husband. Do be brave and self-respecting, and dismiss this creature from your mind and life.[2]

To a girl who hadn't heard from her soldier, Miss Fairfax said: *To write a letter requires some mental effort. To send it requires a two-cent stamp. Believe me, your fickle soldier is worth neither expenditure.*

Her philosophy was simple: *If there's a practical solution, battle for it; if the law will help, invoke the law. In any case, pick up the pieces and keep going.* We have heard this same voice from the Lederer sisters, Eppie and Effie, who wrote advice columns as Ann Landers and Abigail Van Buren. It's the voice of Dr. Laura and Dr. Phil and many others who have followed Beatrice Fairfax.

She was the first Miss Lonely Hearts, celebrated in cartoons, vaudeville, and silent movies; George and Ira Gershwin mentioned her in a song; but she gave it all up in 1905 to marry and settle into what she hoped would be a life without personal problems. As it turned out, real life happened to her, too. Disaster struck her husband, and she had to ask for help herself, and relied on every bit of wisdom good friends could offer.

—ᗰ—

Some of the best advice can be found in the Proverbs—advice for aching hearts, adventurous hearts, misbegotten hearts, mistrusting and all-too-trusting, wandering and wondering hearts. According to tradition, many of these proverbs were authored by Solomon, who knew all about misguided love affairs.

He had been born to the scandalous union of David and Bathsheba. Like his father, Solomon delighted in women; he used marriages to consolidate his power, kept scores of concubines, and famously, Oedipally, courted a Queen of Sheba. Said to be fabulously wealthy, he spent seven years building a great temple for the Lord with slave labor, then another thirteen years building an even greater palace for himself. His fabled wisdom may have been another name for political cunning, for he dispatched his enemies ruthlessly.

In other words, he may have written these proverbs, or he could just as easily have been their cautionary example.

"Do not be wise in your own eyes," warns the third chapter.

"Happy are those who find wisdom, and those who get understanding, for her income is better than silver, and her revenue better than gold. She is more precious than jewels, and nothing you desire can compare with her."

Wisdom, in these proverbs, is feminine—a wife—which is curious, considering Solomon's many liaisons. "King Solomon loved many foreign women along with the daughter of Pharaoh . . . . When Solomon was old, his wives turned away his heart after other gods; and his heart was not true to the LORD his God, as was the heart of his father David." (1 Kings 11:1, 4.)

So when Proverbs inveighs against adultery—it is the book's most sustained alarm—it may be referring to Solomon's religious infidelity; all the more ironic because these words are put in Solomon's mouth.

> A prostitute's fee is only a loaf of bread, but the wife of another stalks a man's very life. Can fire be carried in the bosom without burning one's clothes? Or can one walk on hot coals without scorching the feet? So is he who sleeps with his neighbor's wife; no one who touches her will go unpunished. (Proverbs 6:26–29)

Would a son of Bathsheba really have said this? But then the whole idea of Proverbs is subversive—a king mocked by his own wisdom; his own good advice, excellent advice, at the service of political satire.

Proverbs' three other contributors strike notes at odds with the king's reputation. The very humble Agur says, "Surely I am too stupid to be human; I do not have human understanding. I have not learned wisdom, nor have I knowledge of the holy ones . . . ." King Lemuel's mother counsels, "Do not give your strength to women, your ways to those who destroy kings." And the book ends with an ode to a capable wife.

There could be no more pointed criticism—or poignant self-criticism—than this book. Maybe, just maybe, Solomon did write it in a remorseful old age. We may imagine him in this magnificent palace, jewels winking from the eyes of bronze bulls, servants standing nearby unable to ease the loneliness in his heart. He had been born to immense privilege, had won many women, vast wealth and power, and a reputation for wisdom—but had not been wise enough. In his heart he knew that the kingdom would fracture on his death precisely because of his foolishness. As the shortened proverb has it, pride goeth before a fall.

—⁂—

We know what it's like to be mocked by our own wisdom, to have our own advice thrown back upon us. ("Doubtless you will quote to me this proverb, 'Physician, heal thyself.'") Life upends us even if we have not been particularly proud.

For every mistake we make, there is a maxim to remind us what we should have done differently. We may as well own up to these lessons, of course. But the danger of proverbs, biblical or otherwise, is that they do not know us. We need someone who does, who can help us to balance responsibility with grace.

Strangely enough, we find that gracious friend in the Bible. He is not just two thousand years old, but very much alive, modern. He knows you personally, and his relationship with you is not confined to the page. Solomon may be dead and gone (although his story is ageless); Jesus, however, is not a story. Shut the book and he is still there. Open it again, and he speaks and listens to you.

He speaks right to your anxiety: "Consider the lilies of the field, how they grow; they neither toil nor spin; yet I tell you, even Solomon in all his glory was not clothed like one of these." He laments that a comparative few have come for what he offers: "The Queen of the South will rise up with this generation at the judgment and will condemn it, because she came from the ends of the earth to hear the wisdom of Solomon; and behold, something greater than Solomon is here."

Chiefly, his wisdom is that he knows you. He knows what make your circumstances unique, just as he knew how to answer a rich young man or a much-married woman. And then he offers something even greater.

After three years of answering people's problems, Jesus promised his friends that they would have another counselor. He would not leave them alone.

> I will pray the Father, and he will give you another Counselor, to be with you for ever, even the Spirit of truth, whom the world cannot receive, because it neither sees him nor knows him; you know him, for he dwells with you, and will be in you. (John 14:16–17 RSV)

Consider what this meant in the days just after his death to the timid men from the Galilee, utterly alone and hunted by the authorities. Yes, the resurrection gave them courage, but it didn't completely change them: soon they drifted back to the Galilee and their old jobs. Even after the risen Christ gathered them again, "they worshiped him; but some doubted." No, something else changed them from mere disciples into apostles.

They were provincial men, out of their element in Jerusalem, yet somehow they lost their fear of death, stood up to powerful opponents, and ventured out, alone, to places like Spain, Britain, and India. Apart from the Spirit, it's impossible to explain how this ragtag twelve brought about a worldwide church. The Spirit is central to the Christian faith—as important as the Cross. The one redeems us, and the other remakes us.

All this is absolutely essential because the Christian life so often runs counter to received wisdom. Jesus called those disciples to abandon just about everything that was familiar to them. They could not have done so alone. Maybe you can live by bromides for a while, but when Christ calls you to something beyond common sense—to forgive extravagantly, not to resist evil, not to worry about tomorrow but give up all you have today—well, you'll need the Spirit. If you are going to follow Christ's advice, it will take strength beyond your own head and heart.

—〰—

As I said, Marie Manning went through her own hardships, not long after stepping down from the paper. She didn't mind at first that the woman who took over Beatrice Fairfax's column from her turned out to be cloying and sentimental. A proud woman, six feet tall, Marie had married well and enjoyed family life in a comfortable home in Washington, far from stress and worry.

Then in 1929, the stock market crashed, and her husband lost everything. They were tens of thousands of dollars in debt. Marie was forced to go back to work. Arthur Brisbane, not missing a trick, gave her her old job at the New York *Journal.*

By now the Beatrice Fairfax column was running in two hundred newspapers, and the problems that the readers brought her were serious. Throughout the Depression they wrote her about joblessness; then in World War II, they wanted her to help locate servicemen missing in action. Unwed girls who had gotten pregnant before sending their men off to war needed something other than a witty scolding. In her autobiography, Marie Manning wrote, "We women have learned, even though we vote and hold office, that we can't escape problems or even suffering."

It was a very anxious period indeed; one of her sons served overseas. Friends helped Marie sort through the voluminous mail. Sometimes there were practical solutions, and sometimes there weren't. Sometimes Beatrice Fairfax could meet a dilemma head-on, and sometimes she came up against the limits that her great-uncle Cardinal Manning had faced in the confessional.

"What then is our duty?" Cardinal Manning had once asked. "Not to lament the past nor to dream of the future, but to accept the present. Dreams and lamentations weaken the sinews of action. . . . We must learn the duty and the necessity of seeing things as they are, in their exact and naked truth."[3]

Certain problems lend themselves to tart common sense, whereas Jesus's advice depends on grace. It requires strength we don't possess ourselves—strength from a spirit of wisdom and truth. Lonely hearts, take heart; something greater than Solomon is here.

Remember Me

*T*oday we remember one of the greatest men in history—that great explorer, that famous benefactor, that doer of deeds never to be forgotten, Dr. William Gibson.

This wise and selfless man was passing through the small town of Jamestown, Pennsylvania, one day when he decided to stay and open an apothecary, and began offering, for a small price, a miracle cure for urinary ailments. As specimen vials and money came addressed to "the Water Doctor," he dumped their contents, untested, in a vat outside his office, sent out his miracle powder, and made a small fortune.

Some jealous people called him a quack, and the townspeople really didn't like that vat of urine outside his store, but that didn't stop him from becoming the local postmaster. When he saw another opportunity, he founded the Jamestown and Franklin Railroad. With the capital from those ventures, he established the local bank. Having locked up most of the business in town, he also built a private school for women and opened an opera house.

Of course, an important man like Dr. Gibson required no ordinary house. He and his wife moved into a thirteen-room mansion that dominated the downtown.

In 1867 the Gibsons joined an excursion to Europe and the Holy Lands that included Mark Twain. Dr. Gibson, who had promised to bring back some rare plants for the Smithsonian Institution, traveled under a title he had given himself, *Commissioner of the United States of America to Europe, Asia, and Africa.* Twain wrote,

28

"To my thinking, when the United States considered it necessary to send a dignitary of that tonnage across the ocean, it would be in better taste, and safer, to take him apart and cart him over in sections in several ships." [4]

Gibson was like a character out of Twain, but absurdly actual, terribly real. Twain considered him "an innocent old ass who eats for four and looks wiser than the whole Academy of France . . . and never uses a one-syllable word when he can think of a longer one . . . that serene, that inspired, that overpowering humbug." Twain's pen caught him one day trying to compete with a Mediterranean sunset: "Well, that's gorgis, ain't it! They don't have one of them things in our parts, *do* they? I consider that them effects is on account of the superior refragability, as you might say, of the sun's dirambic combination with the lymphatic forces of the perihelion of Jubiter."[5]

Now, every great man wants to be remembered. Dr. Gibson thought about founding a college. He also donated to the Presbyterian Church a pulpit supposedly made out of African teak from his travels; parishioners discovered it was local lumber.

In the end he decided on erecting a monument for himself, commensurate with his character and accomplishments. It is the largest private memorial in the United States. A bronze lion guards the twelve-step staircase to the tomb. The base of the tomb itself is almost fourteen feet square, and then the pedestal goes up seventy feet—that's taller than a seven-story building—topped by a fifteen-foot statue of Hope.

In 1884, Dr. Gibson ordered this monument at a cost of $100,000. It was shipped from Maine on his own railroad, the Jamestown and Franklin Railroad, and when it arrived, they say, he took a hammer and chipped the top of the statue so that he might have the price discounted for damage in transit.

—᭙—

At the other end of history is a man who may have been homeless, who left no written word, made nothing with his hands that survives; by the usual measure of things, it's as if he never lived.

He spent most of his short life in an area about half the size of Rhode Island, far from any major city. After an obscure youth and wayward adulthood, he was convicted of several crimes and executed.

And that should have been the end of his name. But within days of his death, it was on a great many lips, then spread throughout the country, and soon around the world. I haven't yet mentioned his name, but every one of us knows it. Isn't it, really, a miracle that we all immediate recognize it?

But imagine if he had never lived.

Imagine a world without his stories, or stories about him— where physical laws and ordinary expectations always had the last word; where kingdom, power, and glory belonged only to dictators. Where the poor would be only the poor, rather than three billion different faces for him.

It is amazing and lovely that we remember this man before all others. As the apostle Paul put it:

> Though he was in the form of God, did not count equality with God a thing to be grasped, but emptied himself, taking the form of a servant, being born in the likeness of men. And being found in human form he humbled himself and became obedient unto death, even death on a cross.
>
> Therefore God has highly exalted him and bestowed on him the name which is above every name, that at the name of Jesus every knee should bow, in heaven and on earth and under the earth, and every tongue confess that Jesus Christ is Lord, to the glory of God the Father. (Philippians 2:6–11 RSV)

We remember someone else, too, from that same time. He wasn't very good at his job, because he was caught red-handed at it—convicted of it and sentenced to death. We don't know what he tried to steal. No one kept track of his trial or recorded his name. He should have been forgotten with everyone else from his last day.

Instead, by the grace of God, he wound up on a cross beside the first man. There someone overheard him, in the last moments of his life, as all his foolishness and pettiness drained out of him. He seemed to be thinking clearly for the first time as he said, "Jesus, remember me when you come into your kingdom!"

How presumptuous! A common criminal!

And Jesus said to him, "Truly, I tell you, today you will be with me in Paradise."

—〜〜—

We all want to be remembered. By whom, we're really not sure—maybe by the neighbors or the folks who wander past our monuments in the cemetery a hundred years hence. Perhaps it's pride, or the fear of death, but we want something of us to survive in our work and our children. (Now that a young girl has my last name, I look in her eyes every day to see some of myself, my values, all the while knowing in my dark heart that she is her own person.)

But really it doesn't matter what we do—we are all destined to pass into oblivion. Even the famous among us will be lost, for no one will remember any of us as we really were. As Mark Twain said,

> What a wee part of a person's life are his acts and his words! His real life is led in his head, and is known to none but himself. All day long the mill of his brain is grinding, and his thoughts, not those other things, are his history. Biographies are but the clothes and buttons of the man—the biography of the man himself cannot be written.[6]

But even though the world has never really known us, by the grace of God we are indeed fully known, and will never be forgotten by the one who made us.

In the incredible words of scripture, we have been fearfully and wonderfully made; God has written our names upon the palm of his hand, and even the hairs on our heads have been numbered. Still we hurry on, busying ourselves, anxiously unaware that someone pays attention to the least of us, just as he did to a long-ago thief, with absolutely no concern for who we are or what we've done.

—〜〜—

And what of Dr. William Gibson? Well, he had no children to inherit that vast rambling house. Within a generation it was known not as the Gibson House but as Mark Twain Manor, and it became an inn, then a restaurant. At present it is vacant, gone to rack and ruin. The women's school and the bank closed seventy years ago. The opera house is no longer used. The monument that Gibson built to himself still stands, a curiosity attended to mostly by pigeons.

But if you drive out in the country some ways, you're likely to see in some farmer's field three crosses. They may not rise very high, but they have much to say about life and death. Only one of those crosses is truly tragic. It is like any number of crosses over the graves of those who died trusting in their accomplishments.

The other two, the crosses of humble men, speak of the kingdom, power, and glory.

God help me, I am nailed to my cross. *Jesus, remember me when you come into your kingdom.*

A Conversation

Mary Rodgers lay in the living room, in a hospital bed, dying of cancer. She could no longer get out of bed, but had all her feeding and evacuating done by catheters and pans. Yet her mind was as sharp as ever—she could recite poetry by heart.

And her heart was as full, no, fuller than ever. She knew what she was leaving behind, and gripped Rod Rodgers's hand tightly each ten minutes or so as he checked on her needs. He had been a doctor for forty-five years, had delivered most of the babies in town for two generations, and had alleviated a lot of suffering, though he could not do much now for Mary except well up and cry into his mustache while their daughter changed her sheets. He had always been odd, abrupt, prone to sudden changes in temper, and now he seemed utterly lost. We hardly knew who would die first. They had shared so much together as husband and wife, as parents, as intrepid world travelers who had climbed mountains in Nepal, dug with archaeologists in Turkey, explored Thailand, and followed the Amazon River.

When I saw her every few days, she shared another story of their adventures, or recited poetry, or asked to have some read, such as "Otherwise," by Jane Kenyon:

> I got out of bed
> on two strong legs.
> It might have been
> otherwise. I ate

cereal, sweet
milk, ripe, flawless
peach. It might
have been otherwise.
I took the dog uphill
to the birch wood.
All morning I did
the work I love.

At noon I lay down
with my mate. It might
have been otherwise.
We ate dinner together
at a table with silver
candlesticks. It might
have been otherwise.
I slept in a bed
in a room with paintings
on the walls, and
planned another day
just like this day.
But one day, I know,
it will be otherwise.[7]

One day in January she died. Doc Rodgers was absolutely
beside himself with grief. For quite a while thereafter he tried to
outrun his grief, traveling cross-country and back home, and out
again, and back again, but he had traveled so much with Mary that
he couldn't bear doing it without her.

It took me by surprise to see him again after a long absence, and
so cheerful. He said, "I talked with Mary last night." He described
a vivid conversation in which she had asked if he was eating prop-
erly, and had told him to look in the upper right cabinet above the
microwave for some Ralston. It would help him get his appetite
back. And there it was.

His mental state had always been fragile. Had he gone over the
edge? Perhaps this conversation was a metaphor for his adjustment
to grief. Or perhaps he had had a legitimate vision of her, a true
visit from the afterlife.

—℩ll⁄—

Have you ever had a dream in which a dead loved one spoke to you and seemed alive? We often have dreams that we know are dreams—even as we dream them we say, "This is a dream"—but we also have moments that seem so totally real that after waking we remain convinced of them. Even in broad daylight some people have such moments, so genuine, the details so true, that the only word for them is *numinous:* they put us in the presence of God.

This is a mystery as profound as death itself and life itself, the conversations across the two.

The story of the Transfiguration comes from the middle period of Jesus's ministry, shortly after Peter recognized him as the Christ. Jesus and James and John and Peter went up a sacred mountain, and there the disciples experienced the numinous: they found themselves among the heroes of the faith, Moses and Elijah, and their own companion and living Lord was revealed as the presence of God.

> Jesus took with him Peter and James and John, and led them up a high mountain apart, by themselves. And he was transfigured before them, and his clothes became dazzling white, such as no one on earth could bleach them. And there appeared to them Elijah with Moses who were talking with Jesus. Then Peter said to Jesus, "Rabbi Master, it is good for us to be here; let us make three dwellings, one for you, one for Moses, and one for Elijah." He did not know what to say, for they were terrified. Then a cloud overshadowed them, and from the cloud there came a voice, "This is my Son, the Beloved; listen to him!" Suddenly, when they looked around, they saw no one with them any more, only Jesus. (Mark 9:2–8)

There is no record that the disciples heard any of this conversation, merely that they saw it. So awed were they that they might just as well have been deaf. Peter alone tried to join their conversation and babbled about making dwellings. Dwellings! As if you could capture such an experience!

Perhaps we too would want to say something, anything. If you were Peter, James, or John—or rather, if you beheld not Moses or

Elijah, but someone you knew and loved, what would you say? Perhaps such encounters are always possible; such presences may always be around us, unheard because of grief and disbelief.

A cloud overshadowed them, and from the cloud there came a voice,
   "This is my Son, the Beloved; listen to him!"

—⟋⟍—

We may know more about grief than any people before us. We know about the five stages of grief. We put our loved ones in the care of hospice and ourselves on antidepressants. And yet, separated from death by soft music and flowers, by the people who remove our dead for us, by a consumer culture that ends in walnut caskets, by euphemisms and our own restlessness, we cannot face it as it is.

I have heard brave people reassure me that they have said their good-byes, that they're not worried about Harold anymore, that they'll be okay once they've gotten through the first year. They are in for a rude shock. Grief is not a phase.

It is a conversation. Much to our surprise, we find ourselves talking and talking, and don't know why. Everywhere we go, we talk to our loved ones about milestones and even ordinary irritations and pleasures.

We talk to ourselves, chastising, encouraging, and listening to ourselves as if we were two people—which, in fact, we now are. And we talk to God with an intimacy and urgency we have never known before. Sometimes just a few words suffice: *Why? Now what? How?* Like Peter, we may babble about dwellings: *What should I do about the house? Where should I live?*

And we listen. An uncanny silence inhabits chairs, closets, and coffee cups, a silence that sometimes speaks with the voices of our loved ones. Over and again these halting exchanges express a love very much alive.

That is why I say grief is a conversation. It continues and intensely deepens love.

—៧៧—

Such a conversation can begin before death comes. Jesus prepared his friends for his departure by giving them bread and wine in which they could feel his presence; they could taste and drink his love. He also promised them the Holy Spirit, a comforter. "A little while, and you will no longer see me, and again a little while, and you will see me," he said. "Very truly, I tell you, you will weep and mourn, but the world will rejoice; you will have pain, but your pain will turn into joy. . . . So you have pain now; but I will see you again, and your hearts will rejoice, and no one will take your joy from you." (John 16:16, 20, 22.)

Iris Murdoch, one of the greatest novelists in the English language, suffered in her last years from Alzheimer's. Her husband, the critic John Bayley, set aside his writing career to feed, bathe, and dress her. One morning he came upon a slip in her bureau which he recognized from their courtship forty years before. She had saved this memento from a day they had gone swimming in a river. It was "stiff with powdery traces of dry mud. It is faded to a yellowish color; a wrinkled ribbon, once blue, decorates the hem. Could someone, later my wife, once have worn such a garment? It looks like something preserved from the wardrobe of Marie Antoinette."[8]

This relic of their intimacy moved him deeply. He felt overwhelmed by all the things they once had taken for granted. So much can go unsaid in a marriage or remain at the sea bottom until great tectonic shifts bring everything to the surface. These changes brought him grief and joy. Where once he took pride in her vigorous mind, now he took solace in sympathy and understanding. Where once he and Iris delighted in language, now they took pleasure in what could be said without words. He wrote, "Life is no longer bringing us 'closer and closer apart,' in A.D. Hope's tenderly ambiguous words. Every day, we move closer and closer together. We could not do otherwise."

But he would not romanticize the loss, and observed,

There is a certain comic irony—happily, not darkly, comic—
that, after more than forty years of our taking marriage for

granted, marriage has decided it is tired of this and is taking a hand in the game. Purposefully, persistently, involuntarily, our marriage is now getting somewhere. It is giving us no choice, and I am glad of that.[9]

—ᴍ—

Let's be clear about what grief is not. Grief is not a phase. That is an insensitive and insulting idea, for we feel real losses for the rest of our lives. Grief is not a mental disturbance, nor a mere hurdle. It is not a passing storm.

Grief is a conversation. When we talk about the communion of the saints, we mean that in a very real sense they are present, attentive, and even responsive. Even people who say they don't believe in an afterlife behave as if they do, because love has such power. Love means sharing our strongest feelings, so those conversations will continue. It could not be otherwise.

The voices are all around us. They speak to us from sock drawers and cupboards and notes left in books years ago. They would visit us sleeping and waking.

Listen to her. Listen to them: to the sensible voices of loved ones whose perspectives are now unimaginably wide. God knows what it's like to grieve, and also knows what's on the other side. From the cloud of grief there comes a voice saying, *"This is my Son, my beloved child. Listen to him."* We should begin a conversation there, too.

Handel's Messiah

Georg was a complicated boy. His father thought music a trifle, a waste of intelligence, but his mother helped him to smuggle a clavichord into the attic, where he could practice secretly. By age six he had mastered the instrument, and within a few years he could also play the violin, harpsichord, oboe, and organ.

Dutifully following his father's wishes, Georg studied law, though he hated it. But after his father died, he left his native Germany, traveled widely, and became a master of Italian music, particularly opera. Oddly enough, Italian music was extremely popular in Germany and England. When one of his patrons, a German duke, became England's king, Georg Friedrich Handel followed him there and founded an Italian opera company. As one would imagine, this German-English composer of Italian music was a complicated man.

Even his friends thought so. "He was in his person a large-made and very portly man," said one. "His gait, which was ever sauntering, was rather ungraceful, as it had a rocking motion, which distinguishes those whose legs are bowed." Another recalled, "His general look was somewhat heavy and sour; but when he did smile, it was the sun bursting out of a black cloud."

Handel claimed that knowing the Bible like a bishop gave him strength. No doubt he needed it, for running the opera house proved to be a great deal of trouble. In 1737, after overwork and exhaustion, he suffered a stroke and paralysis, which took away his skill, his genius, as a performer. He tried again to compose in the Italian vein, but tastes were changing, and two of his operas failed to please audiences in London.

Handel had run short of money; creditors dogged him. At the age of fifty-six, he shut himself in his house, dejected and alone, and prepared to return to Germany.

Then he received a new libretto, in English, drawn from the Bible, about the Savior, the suffering servant by whose stripes we are healed. The first part told of Christ's Advent and his birth; the second, of his Passion and triumphant Resurrection, ending with an Hallelujah chorus; and the third part, of a Resurrection for all humankind.

The texts gave him heart, gave him purpose. Day and night he worked, often ignoring the meals brought to him by servants. A friend called upon Handel when he was setting to music the words *He was despised and rejected of men,* and found him "absolutely sobbing." He was so moved by the Hallelujah chorus that he put the words in his journal, and of it he later said, paraphrasing Paul in Second Corinthians, "Whether I was in my body or out of my body as I wrote it, I know not. God knows." Amazingly he finished the *Messiah* in a mere three weeks.

Finances desperately thin, he took a job in Dublin and brought with him the score, but he refused to premiere the *Messiah* for his own gain; now and for the rest of his life, it would raise money for charity. The premiere took place at the Dublin Cathedral on April 13, 1742, a benefit concert for the "prisoners of several jails, for Mercer's Hospital, and for the Charitable Infirmary," and the musicians performed for free. The audience numbered seven hundred in a church built for six hundred. Mrs. Susannah Cibber, who had been disgraced in an adulterous relationship three years before, sang the contralto part. After she sang of Christ's sufferings, the chancellor of the cathedral rose and cried, "Woman, for this, all thy sins be forgiven thee!"

The work was a great success. Since its premiere, there has never been a year in which the *Messiah* has not been performed. It is the most popular work in the classical repertoire, perhaps the most popular music the world has ever known.

In 1749 and for years afterwards, Handel performed the *Messiah* for London's Foundling Hospital, which cared for children who had been abandoned. This immense and sometimes difficult man, removed from the country of his birth, partially paralyzed on his left side, with cataracts in both eyes, had no children of his own. Yet through him the *Messiah* came to the foundlings.

—꿰—

Handel's messiah was born in a small town to obscure parents who may have traveled more than a hundred miles on foot in the last weeks of his mother's pregnancy. Apparently there were questions about who really was the boy's father. He was a Semitic boy who spoke a language known by only a few thousand people in all history. His boyhood is lost to the waters and sands.

Handel's messiah was a man of flesh and blood, hair and hunger, family, shelter, sleep, and work. He was a human being. Whether or not he was also the eternal God, the Creator of all that he now touched, he was certainly a human being. Companions who traveled with him for three years wondered aloud at what sort of man he was, yet he sought out retreats in quiet places because he, like they, grew weary. When his friends died, he wept.

Handel's messiah died at a young age, even though he very much wanted to live. Despite seeing the sadness and baseness of this world, he loved it very much, and loved nothing better than sitting down at a table with friends. He was acclaimed as a teacher, a rabbi, a prophet, a king, yet he gave up every title and position, and then gave up much more than that.

When he died, many of those closest to him thought he had accomplished absolutely nothing. No one would have thought of setting this life to music.

And yet soon after his death, many people did write down that life, and its holiness made those pages scripture. Handel's *Messiah* came straight from scripture. He was not a character created by a librettist; the words of the oratorio came from the Bible, and the portrait is timeless and true.

Comfort ye, comfort ye my people, saith your God; speak ye
comfortably to Jerusalem; and cry unto her, that her warfare is
accomplished, that her iniquity is pardoned. The voice of him
that crieth in the wilderness, Prepare ye the way of the Lord,
make straight in the desert a highway for our God.

Every valley shall be exalted, and every mountain and hill made
low; the crooked straight, and the rough places plain. And the
glory of the Lord shall be revealed, and all flesh shall see it
together.

The people that walked in darkness have seen a great light: and
they that dwell in the land of the shadow of death, upon them
has the light shined. For unto us a Child is born, unto us a Son
is given, and the government shall be upon His shoulder: and
His name shall be called Wonderful, Counselor, the Mighty
God, the Everlasting Father, the Prince of Peace.

The words themselves are musical, the very summit of Hebrew and
Greek poetry, but they were not written for the pleasure of their
sound. They testify to a music beyond the hearing of ears, an order
and beauty from another realm. We would do the scriptures a dis-
service simply to applaud them; they want us to be moved by their
subject. Indeed, they introduce us to someone who lived a stub-
bornly human life. Listen:

Surely He hath borne our griefs, and carried our sorrows; He
was wounded for our transgressions; He was bruised for our
iniquities; the chastisement of our peace was upon Him. And
with His stripes we are healed.

—ᴍ—

The man who put this other man's life to music inspired various
feelings. Joseph Haydn is said to have "wept like a child" at the
Hallelujah chorus. Mozart is said to have remarked, "Handel
understands effect better than any of us—when he chooses, he
strikes like a thunderbolt." Beethoven said, "Handel is the greatest
composer that ever lived. . . . I would uncover my head and kneel

down on his tomb." Hector Berlioz, however, called Handel "a tub of pork and beer."

Yes, he was a complicated man. He could swear in five languages. Once he threatened to throw a soprano out a window. And yet he had the physical courage to endure three operations on his eyes at the hands of the same surgeon who had unsuccessfully operated on Johann Sebastian Bach, and the spiritual courage to accept the same result—complete blindness. Even then he continued to perform.

An Englishwoman, deeply moved by the *Messiah,* asked him how it was possible for him, "who understood the English language imperfectly, to enter so fully into the sublime spirit of the words." Handel answered, "Madam, I thank God I have a little religion."

He hoped to die on Good Friday so that he might rise with his Christ on Easter Sunday. In April of 1759, Handel collapsed following another charity performance of his great work. As it turned out, he died on Maundy Thursday.

Though he had had no children of his own, he felt so deeply about them that in his will he left the *Messiah* to the Foundling Hospital.

—⟊—

The word *messiah* is not a personal name, and yet it has very personal implications.

Handel's messiah could hear the plight of an overage, overweight German lost in another country, broke, discouraged. He could make a sick old man a holy person, redeemed and revived. Handel's messiah was not a mere work of music, but a man.

Who is your messiah? Is there someone who knows you as no one else does, and still loves you more than anyone else? Is there someone who makes sense, even art, of your discordant life?

There is. Beyond music, there is a man; and beyond the man, there is a messiah—for all the lostlings and all the foundlings.

Hidden in Plain Sight

*T*his is how Christmas arrived one year, ahead of schedule, on a Friday afternoon with a nine-year-old girl and her mother.

They lived in a trailer behind a gas station, close to a bunch of other trailers and a pole barn. Mud was everywhere. The big trucks that pulled into the gas station had left ruts in the patchy grass.

I came calling just after lunch, when lots of cars were there, lots of little dogs barking, and a little blonde girl with grown-up eyes came to the door. That wasn't her mother behind her, nor was the other woman. They were in-laws, there to help Becky, who was in the kitchen. Maybe ten people were in that narrow trailer. These folks hadn't seen each other much over the years, and their tension couldn't be erased even though everyone was trying to help, because they had been brought together by tragedy.

Earlier in the week, Becky's husband, Jason, who had just been served with divorce papers, had barricaded himself in the pole barn he had built next door. For hours, with police all around, he had threatened to kill himself; and at last he did. The family was convinced that it was an accident, that Jason had been crying for help and only meant to injure himself instead of leaving them like this.

And now it was two weeks before Christmas. We talked awhile about the funeral service, about how Whitney was doing. (She quickly vanished and came back out once or twice.) There were some funny stories from happier times. Cigarette smoke and the aroma of coffee filled the trailer as we went over the good and the not-so-good history. Becky seemed relieved to be talking about this with someone, at last.

Would it be all right if some folks from my church got a Christmas gift for Whitney? Becky's eyes were not used to letting on her emotions. That would be wonderful, she said, and held her gaze on me as she said it a second time.

About the only thing Whitney wanted that day was to turn invisible. She didn't need a lot of people hovering over her, and she certainly wasn't ready to be a victim. This may have been the worst, but it wasn't the first, blow in her life. As soon as an aunt pressed a few dollars in her hand, she leapt from the front door, not touching the steps, and took off across the lot for the gas station.

You couldn't help but wonder what she would face at school. Kids like her don't think poorly of themselves, not all the time, although an ordinary school day can be enough to remind them where they come from. Maybe you remember from your own childhood. You know where to find these kids. After school, for example, you probably wouldn't look for them on the soccer field in uniform, or in the library. They might be at home alone, or might be elsewhere, alone.

I don't know where you're looking for the Christ child, but believe me—she's hidden in plain sight.

—⁓—

The Christ child came when hardly any in his country were looking. We do not get the sense that hundreds or thousands searched the skies or even noticed angels or a star. A few astronomers in a distant country did, but not his countrymen. The innkeeper surely didn't notice anything in the sky. We do not sense that many people in Bethlehem paid attention to his birth, even though it was a very small town.

When those astronomers arrived in Jerusalem, probably long after the birth, and asked where they might find the messiah, king of the Jews, King Herod, a very poor Jew, had to ask his advisors. "In Bethlehem, of course," they all told him, for so it was written by the prophets. Herod, who had been king of the Jews up till now, was determined not to let his rival reach adulthood. He told the wise men to go and search for the child, and then to bring word back to him; but his treachery must have been too obvious, for they never returned.

Herod was furious, but really for what cause? The child was hidden in plain sight. How hard could it have been to find a young boy in Bethlehem?

—◊—

How hard could it be today to find the Christ child?

Apparently, not everyone is looking. Many people do not seem to notice the portents in the night sky, or even that the sun has gone down. They are too busy carrying out their lives—running their inns or their shops, buying gifts, or preparing for company—to notice the nine-year-old girl in a trailer park or to make room for her in their imaginations.

It could be easy to miss her this time of year, what with all our shopping. After all, she's probably not hanging around the stores where we would hope to find something special.

On the other hand, it must take quite a mental effort to forget her altogether. Unemployment in my town stands at 9 percent. Canned goods are flying off the shelves of the food pantry; folks have to choose between heat and food, what with the price of natural gas going up and the minimum delivery costing hundreds of dollars. The director of the pantry says, "This problem is not faceless. These are people we all know—from our families, our church families, the children our children go to school with. . . . It's all around us, and if you don't think of someone right away, you're probably not thinking very hard."

They seem so earthbound, so terribly human. Maybe God deliberately appeared among the working poor rather than the privileged so we would see them as God sees them and discover their dignity and love. The incarnation forces us to look there for our salvation.

We look for saviors in all kinds of places: among men in tailored suits whose exploits are told in financial magazines, and women in workout videos and syndicated talk shows, and authority figures of all kinds. But we rarely think to look for our savior in someone in need, even though Jesus said, "Whenever you care for the least of my people, behold, you do so for me."

So let's go up the road to the frame house with the rotting siding and the Dodge truck rusting on the lawn. Dad has been laid off from an auto parts supplier; Mom is going back to school in hopes of getting a hospital job. The three kids have been forced to grow up quickly—a little too quickly—and sometimes they get into trouble. Every Sunday, though, they all come to church together and borrow a little strength for the week. Amazingly, when there's a crisis with another family, they are the first to respond with a dish or a homemade coffeecake.

The holy family would seem just as unlikely to show the way to salvation. Mary and Joseph weren't married when their first child was born. Without a place to stay, they had to do the best they could with a makeshift cradle. Then they jerked the child around from place to place—Bethlehem, then Egypt, then Nazareth. At some point Joseph disappeared from the boy's life; we don't know why. Jesus had differences with his mother and siblings. In fact, early in his ministry when they came to take him home, he turned to his disciples and asked, "Who are my mother and my brothers?"

Yet when he hung on the cross, his mother was there; Jesus even asked his closest friend to take her as his mother. And his brother James bravely took charge of the disciples after Jesus was gone.

The strengths of this family must have been apparent to visitors from the very beginning. Having spent their careers among jaded and dangerous royalty, the wise men could appreciate people who trusted God and truly loved each other. When they came to Bethlehem, they had an epiphany, a revelation.

The shepherds needed some instructions from an angel as to where their savior lay, for they wouldn't have thought to look for the king of the Jews in such a humble place. They would have walked right by him. The angel said, *This will be a sign for you:*

you will find a child wrapped in bands of cloth and lying in a manger. Sure enough, he was in plain sight.

And what a blessing he was! What a miracle to find salvation in this child! It changes us to meet people living out the beatitudes—to discover that the common are uncommon, the poor are rich, the uneducated wise, the simple complex, the desperate full of hope, the grieving full of life!

—ᴍ—

Three days after we met, Becky took her daughter to the funeral. Whitney wore a black-and-white dress, with her hair pulled back with a barrette. Like her mother, she didn't show much of what she was feeling, but when the service was over and her father's friends were at the casket, another young girl came to sit with her, and then Whitney melted into her mother's arms.

One of my parishioners drove over to the house with some Christmas gifts. No one came to the door. A neighbor happened by and explained that the family had gone to the visitation, that the funeral would begin in an hour, but that the Bay Shore Presbyterian Church was open, and the ladies were setting up in the basement for the funeral luncheon.

My friend walked up the road, dropped off the gifts on tables already full of food. Maybe the packages would be easily spotted, maybe not. No matter.

The road from the church to the gas station, only a couple hundred yards, was muddy, full of holes—holy.

As she walked back down the hill, the gray sky shone on the gray road, and cars whizzed by on the highway. So many cars would pass by there every hour; so few would ever stop.

And yet God was hard at work there. A train of people entered the church carrying casseroles. Arriving cars splashed the puddles. To my friend, just then it looked like the setting for a Christmas story, although the calendar said it was two weeks away.

The Nearest Star

*D*id you see the stars last night? After the snow, they were completely unnecessary, and so all the more beautiful, all the more poised and distant. They put problems on earth in proper perspective.

Many years ago there was a television program in which entertainers sought the advice of a panel on their personal problems. The teen sensation Eddie Fisher complained that chorus girls refused to go out with him because he was so young. George S. Kaufman, one of the panelists, listened for a few moments and said:

"Mr. Fisher, on Mount Wilson there is a telescope that can magnify the most distant stars up to twenty-four times the magnification of any previous telescope. This remarkable instrument was unsurpassed in the world of astronomy until the development and construction of the Mount Palomar telescope—an even more remarkable instrument of magnification. Owing to advances and improvements in optical technology, it is capable of magnifying the stars to four times the magnification and resolution of the Mount Wilson telescope."

Kaufman put his chin on his hand and leaned forward. "Mr. Fisher, if you could somehow put the Mount Wilson telescope *inside* the Mount Palomar telescope, you *still* wouldn't be able to detect my interest in your problem."[10]

I think many of us have felt that way about other people's problems, or have feared that somebody felt that way about our own. We've all heard so many problems.

So many people.

Very young children sometimes hear that for every soul born on earth, there is a star in the night sky. Just look up in the sky, and see if that is consoling. So many stars—more than we can see with the naked eye.

How many stars are there? Well, the astronomer Edwin Hubble, for whom the Hubble telescope is named, determined that we belong to a spiral-shaped galaxy. Our sun is just an ordinary, average-sized star near the inner edge of one of its arms. Hubble figured out the distances to nine other galaxies. We now can see, with modern telescopes, a hundred thousand million other galaxies, each galaxy with about a hundred thousand million stars. To the astronomer, human beings are infinitely small, mere specks in a universe that is vast and dark.

—〰—

This is the world into which Jesus Christ was born. A world of anonymous persons.

King Herod, the Roman ruler of Judea, was the only person of the few millions who mattered. So you can imagine his distress when astronomers from Persia came to pay homage to the newborn king of the Jews. They had seen an unusual star in the East, and, knowing something of the Hebrew scriptures, had realized that it might announce the birth of the messiah.

Herod wasn't much of a Jew; he had to ask his chief priests where the messiah was to be born. They told him, "Bethlehem, of course," a small town only twelve miles from Jerusalem; it had been the home of David, the first great king of the Jews.

This was too close for comfort. Herod called for the astronomers and told them to search for the child—in effect, to be his spies.

These men might have known a prophecy from Isaiah: "The Lord himself will give you a sign. Look, the young woman is with child and shall bear a son, and shall name him Immanuel." (Isaiah 7:14.) The name meant "God is with us." But for Isaiah, it had been less of a promise than a threat that God planned to wreak havoc on Israel:

> Band together, you peoples, and be dismayed; listen, all you far countries; gird yourselves and be dismayed! Take counsel together, but it shall be brought to naught; speak a word, but it will not stand, for God is with us. (Isaiah 8:9–10)

Somehow Matthew, the gospel writer, reclaimed that prophecy as good news. "Look, the virgin will conceive and bear a son, and they shall name him Emmanuel," which means, "God is with us." *(Matthew 1:23.)* More than just the spelling of the name had changed. Here the immanence of God meant good tidings, an answer to mysteries, a powerful blow to Herod's treachery. With it came a sign, paradoxically noticed only by wise men who came from far away, a star signifying that God was near.

That star calls for an explanation. If it wasn't entirely legendary, it might have been a conjunction of planets, Venus and Mercury, maybe, or a comet that crossed the sky that season. But the behavior of this star fascinates me. It wasn't like any other object in the night sky. It *moved*—it *went before* the wise men— and then it stopped. And somehow it stopped above the place where the child lay—so it must have been low enough in the sky to indicate the point precisely. The whole point of the star was that it pointed out the way. If it had been one of the distant heavenly bodies, it couldn't have done that.

What is the nearest star? Schoolchildren will tell you Alpha Centauri, or Proxima Centauri, which is four light-years away. Or the sun, which is eight light-minutes away.

I would suggest that the nearest star is much nearer. It comes out at night—that is, when we confront our problems.

—∿∿—

In January of 1931, Edwin Hubble showed Albert Einstein the Mount Wilson telescope through which he had detected galaxies beyond the Milky Way and had proved that the universe is expanding. "To the astronomer," Hubble said, "man is nothing more than an insignificant dot in an infinite universe." "I have often felt that," Einstein replied. "But then I realize that the insignificant dot who is the man is also the astronomer."

Amazing, isn't it, that in this vast universe there are thinking beings with the gifts of sight and curiosity, and that *we are they.*

A friend of mine in college, grappling with large questions of human meaning, felt that our amusements and passions were absurdly out of proportion to our size in the universe. And then he came to see thing differently. Other nonreligious people have had similar moments. He said, with a touch of wonder, "Maybe we are how the universe knows itself."

Well, that's a possibility. Maybe the story of human life is a big telescope pointing out into the stars.

The gospel, however, suggests something else. It takes my breath away to suggest this: maybe the story of human life is a big telescope pointing back at *us.* If you could somehow put the Mount Wilson telescope *inside* the Mount Palomar telescope, you *still* wouldn't be able to see human life more closely than Christ has seen it, or magnify its importance any more than he has.

There is the possibility that we are infinitely important in God's plan. It is just as scandalous and amazing in our time as it was in the time of Herod. But we must take it seriously if we take the Christmas story seriously.

That is just what Herod feared. In a world of anonymous persons, Herod has infinite power. In a world of persons who are known, and loved, of infinite worth, Herod becomes stripped of power, as naked as a baby.

Herod might not have understood what the star meant, but he knew that he was more comfortable in a night without it. If he had been a better Jew, though, he might have known from the eighth psalm that the God of the heavens pays close attention:

> O Lord, our Sovereign, how majestic is your name in all the earth!
> You have set your glory above the heavens.
>   Out of the mouths of babes and infants you have founded a
>   bulwark. . . .

When I look at your heavens, the work of your fingers,
    the moon and the stars that you have established;
what are human beings that you are mindful of them,
    mortals that you care for them?

(Psalm 8)

At night, when we confront our problems, God draws near. As we lie in bed, there may be no one else awake to listen or reassure us, nothing to distract us from our fears—nothing to see except our imaginings, nothing to do except think. If we try to solve problems all by ourselves, we are in for a long night indeed. But that is when God comes near. As close as can be, God says, *It's just a few more hours to morning. Let's see how things turn out.*

In the light of day, even large problems sometimes seem more manageable. There's no need to make a big deal out of everything. And at night it can be comforting and ennobling to walk out and see stars so beautiful, poised, and distant.

There are other nights when it's comforting and ennobling to think that we, we are seen and known in the sharpest focus—that our passions and amusements, hurts and joys, griefs, longings, loneliness and faith, all are known by someone who sees us close-up, closer than any lens can go. "From your lips to God's ear," says the Hebrew blessing. The heavenly body comes closer, closer, closer, and then we find it smoldering in the hay, in human skin.

What

My Disagreements with Jesus

I have been disagreeing with Jesus for many years now. Usually he expresses my views pretty well, but every once in a while he says something I don't believe. For example, he maintains that if you are angry with a brother or sister, or call someone a fool, you might go to hell. It's hard to imagine that God would make a big deal about *that.* Jesus also says, "Do not think that I have come to bring peace to the earth; I have not come to bring peace, but a sword. For I have come to set a man against his father." An adolescent attempt to sound radical.

I'll admit that Jesus is pretty clever, and he makes more sense to me than he once did, but what do you suppose he means by those mysterious stories where the wrong people come out ahead? It's one thing to honor a good Samaritan, another thing entirely for him to praise a dishonest steward.

There are times I feel Jesus needs to be a little more Christian.

And yet, even though he makes me wince and wonder, I am haunted by the possibility that he could be right. I have hoped that he has been misquoted, misreported, that the more difficult stories have been mangled by the gospel writers. But they might have taken pains to get him exactly right. Maybe the fundamentalists are onto something; maybe this strange and unsettling Jesus is the real Jesus.

—⁓—

He makes me uneasy when he heals people by saying, "You are forgiven." And yet those are indeed healing words. He unnerves me with his repeated warnings about the pitfalls of money, as if they really applied to middle-class people . . . and . . . well, okay, maybe they do. Yes, he seems to take delight in unsettling me, as if he *wants* me to disagree with him; he can be tricky that way, especially when he is talking about the kingdom of God.

And often he does this by telling some objectionable story.

Jesus's parables start out in everyday life, but they don't end up there. At the bottom of every one of them is a trapdoor out of our familiar world and into his kingdom, where the values are upside down. This one, for example, doesn't sound nice at all:

> "It is as if a man, going on a journey, summoned his slaves and entrusted his property to them; to one he gave five talents, to another two, to another one, to each according to his ability. Then he went away. The one who had received the five talents went off at once and traded with them, and made five more talents. In the same way, the one who had the two talents made two more talents. But the one who had received the one talent went off and dug a hole in the ground and hid his master's money. After a long time the master of those slaves came and settled accounts with them. Then the one who had received five talents came forward, bringing five more talents, saying, 'Master, you handed over to me five talents; see, I have made five more talents.' His master said to him, 'Well done, good and trustworthy slave; you have been trustworthy in a few things, I will put you in charge of many things; enter into the joy of your master.' And the one with the two talents came forward, saying. 'Master, you handed over to me two talents; see, I have made two more talents.' His master said to him, 'Well done, good and trustworthy slave; you have been trustworthy in a few things, I will put you in charge of many things; enter into the joy of your master.' Then the one who had received the one talent also came forward, saying, 'Master, I knew that you were a harsh man, reaping where you did not sow, and gathering where you did not scatter seed; so I was afraid, and I went and hid your talent in the ground. Here you have what is yours.' But his master replied, 'You wicked and lazy slave! You knew, did you, that I reap where I

did not sow, and gather where I did not scatter? Then you ought to have invested my money with the bankers, and on my return I would have received what was my own with interest. So take the talent from him, and give it to the one withthe ten talents. For to all those who have, more will be given, and they will have an abundance; but from those who have nothing, even what they have will be taken away. As for this worthless slave, throw him into the outer darkness, where there will be weeping and gnashing of teeth.' " Matthew 25:14–30

Now, this is truly a strange story, and as an American my first instinct is to read it as investment advice. *Look, man, don't stash your money in a mattress! That's disrespectful to money! Make it work for you, earn some interest, or the Boss Man will be displeased!* My first thought, then, is that it can't possibly be about me, because I do invest money and see that it doesn't get wasted.

Well, that is, I give what I can. If you're going to start that crazy business about selling everything and giving the money to the poor, that's another matter. But God gets his standard cut.

That's when we fall through the trap door, pass through the looking glass, and realize that the story is upside-down; that Jesus is not describing the kingdom, but its opposite. We have thought that this Boss Man must be God. But listen to this awful master: *You knew that I reap where I did not sow, and gather where I did not scatter. . . .*

Could this really be God? We may have been taught that God is wrathful and demanding, but if God *isn't* a taskmaster . . . then the Boss Man is *not* God.

Come to think of it, God wouldn't really expect his servants to put money out at interest. In fact he has condemned moneylending among the Jews and has charged us to give to the poor, to care for the widow and orphan. When the Boss Man says, "You ought to have invested my money with the bankers," maybe Jesus is winking at us.

Yes, he is winking. The Boss Man in his story says, "Take the talent from him, and give it to the one with ten talents. For to all those who have, more will be given; and from those who have nothing, even what they have will be taken away." But Jesus has declared that "the first shall be last, and the last shall be first." He has said, "Every mountain shall be made low, and every valley shall be lifted up, and all flesh shall see it together." He has said, "Blessed are you who are poor now, for yours is the kingdom of heaven."

At last it begins to dawn on us who the Boss Man is. He is the Boss Man in our world, and although his standards are the world's standards, they certainly aren't God's.

This parable of the talents appears in the twenty-fifth chapter of Matthew just before Jesus's story of the sheep and the goats, in which all persons are judged by how they have cared for the hungry, the thirsty, the sick and the imprisoned. Both stories are about doing what God expects of us. If we read this parable in reverse— if we understand it as a scathing commentary on worldly values masquerading as religious values—then clearly the way to please God is to give away what we have.

So our first impression was not far wrong. It turns out after all that Jesus *is* offering investment advice—to invest in the poor, for the returns will be great. What we give away will come back with interest. We must give away whatever we can, even if we fear we don't have much. Jesus is speaking directly to those of us whose modest means might keep us from risking and giving: we hoard our small stash at our peril.

Our first impression was right in another way, too—this parable is very unsettling, but we can no longer pretend that it doesn't make sense or that it's not about us.

—m—

Oh, he is skilled at keeping us off balance. Whenever we think we are talking about someone else, he turns the subject back on us, so that we hear our own words and contradictions. Maybe we are a little too quick to disagree with the master, for he courts disagreement the way a jujitsu artist waits for an opponent to lunge, and he even knows how to deflect the murderous argument of the cross: the resurrection is his unanswerable reply.

I have learned over the years of my disagreements with Jesus that he's often finally right. It just takes me a while to find that, yes, peace only comes with forgiveness—from God, from us—and that you really can't love God and Mammon both. It turns out that he is psychologically acute ("Why do you not see the log in your own eye?" he asks, describing transference long before Freud). He is right about letting go of the things no one can keep. He is right about the lilies of the field and not being anxious. He is so profoundly right in some of his most puzzling sayings that I am obliged to give him the benefit of the doubt always. But really, the benefit of the doubt is mine.

And Then It Hits You

*T*his year hasn't been notable for peace or calm, but it has been notable for lightning.

On September 18, a woman in Grand Forks, North Dakota, was struck by lightning while leaving work. For hours afterward she had muscle seizures and twitches, yet she expressed gratitude. Her daughter said, "There definitely was an angel watching over her today."

In August, a woman vacationing in Greece barely escaped death when lightning struck her tongue stud. She was temporarily blinded, blistered all over, and unable to speak for three days.

A woman in Asheboro, North Carolina, was late getting home on the first day of July; just as she pulled into the driveway, her house was hit by a thunderbolt. The outside wall of her kitchen was blown out, the roof fell in, lights exploded, her refrigerator was pierced by a two-by-four. "Can you believe how powerful lightning is?" she said. "I feel very lucky."

You'd feel lucky, too. A bolt of lightning carries anywhere from a hundred million to a billion volts, and can be five times hotter than the sun. The force turns rainwater and body sweat into steam and literally blows clothes off. Yet 90 percent of those hit survive. I've always wondered about people who have been struck by lightning—if perhaps they see things differently, if their hearts beat in a different rhythm. You'd think that their spines would always tingle, that they would live in a state of constant surprise.

It's pleasant to think so, but some folks just don't feel the miracle. Consider the British man who this May was hit *twice* during the same round of golf, on the fourteenth and seventeenth holes. He completed his round, and afterwards all he would say was that he didn't shoot his best.

Also in May, the president of Bulgaria asked experts to investigate why a house had been struck by lightning nine separate times and always at the same hour of the day. The Cholakov family in the southern Bulgarian village of Truncha had installed two lightning rods, to no avail. It always struck between 3:30 and 4:30 in the afternoon. In fright, they had taken to living in a tent in the garden and kept buckets of water on hand in case of fire. Apparently they didn't think their experience was miraculous.

And then I suppose we should consider Roy Sullivan, a forest ranger in Virginia, who was struck seven times. The first strike, in 1942, ripped off his big toenail. Twenty-seven years later, the second one knocked him unconscious and burned his eyebrows off. A year after that, a bolt burned his shoulder. By now he had gotten a reputation, and people called him the Human Lightning Rod; he got a little nervous, too. A strike in 1972 set his hair on fire; after that he always had a pail of water nearby, which came in handy the next year when a bolt tore through his hat, set his hair on fire again, and knocked him out of his truck. The sixth bolt singed his ankle, and the last one, in 1977, burned his upper body. Not a one of them took his life. He took his own life, in 1983.

All those miracles, and that's how the story ended. God's power can strike all around us, and still we might not get it.

—៳៳—

Those who met Jesus didn't immediately feel the effects. Their hair didn't smoke, they didn't give off an electrical charge; in fact they seemed little changed by coming in contact with him. Thousands of people must have come close to him without registering a difference. But there was this one woman who fought through the crowds just to touch him. Weakened and desperate from twelve years of bleeding, she reached out through the thicket of ankles and knees to touch the hem of his robe.

He noticed her. "Who touched me?" he asked. "I felt power go out from me." Oddly, no one else in the jostling crowd had a similar effect on him. Only she had been able to tap his power simply by her need and faith, and did so before he was even aware of her.

It is hard for us to appreciate how alone she was in that crowd. Twelve years of menstrual bleeding had made her ritually impure, and by touching Jesus she had defiled him, too, just as he was going to the home of a synagogue official.

For she had approached Jesus as he was on the way to cure a twelve-year-old girl. Matthew, Mark, and Luke leave the stories knotted together, as "a miracle on the way to a miracle":

> Now when Jesus returned, the crowd welcomed him, for they were all waiting for him. Just then there came a man named Jairus, a leader of the synagogue. He fell at Jesus's feet and begged him to come to his house, for he had an only daughter, about twelve years old, who was dying.
>
> As he went, the crowds pressed in on him. Now there was a woman who had been suffering from hemorrhages for twelve years; and though she had spent all she had on physicians, no one could cure her. She came up behind him and touched the fringe of his clothes, and immediately her hemorrhage stopped. Then Jesus asked, "Who touched me?" When all denied it, Peter said, "Master, the crowds surround you and press in on you." But Jesus said, "Someone touched me; for I noticed that power had gone out from me." When the woman saw that she could not remain hidden, she came trembling; and falling down before him, she declared in the presence of all the people why she had touched him, and how she had been immediately healed. He said to her, "Daughter, your faith has made you well; go in peace."
>
> While he was still speaking, someone came from the leader's house to say, "Your daughter is dead; do not trouble the teacher any longer." When Jesus heard this, he replied, "Do not fear. Only believe. . . ." (Luke 8:40–50)

It's curious, isn't it, that the gospel writers haven't separated these stories? And then it hits you: this woman had been suffering ever since the girl was born. She could even have been the girl's mother. During these years, however, she could not have been intimate with a man, had any relations with a man, or given birth to a child. Ordinary love for her was taboo. Her own body testified to the high cost of bringing life into the world, just as Jesus would show the high cost of preserving it.

Significantly he called her "daughter" in front of the crowd worried for Jairus's daughter. She was the only woman in the gospels whom he addressed this way. The term itself, in that place and moment, must have been healing. Her sexual stigma became innocence again, and just as surely as he restored the child, he raised this grown woman to new life. "Daughter," he said, "your faith has made you well; go in peace."

The more we read of the gospels, the more remarkable her faith becomes. Five thousand people ate from five loaves and two fish, but retreated to disbelief. Ten lepers were healed, but only one returned to give thanks. Even the disciples fell away.

Now, there are medical explanations for this. One of the symptoms of being struck by God's blessings, of course, is memory loss. We forget the marvelous things that God gives almost as soon as we receive them. We are so affected by God's overwhelming power that we develop ear problems, eye problems. Sometimes I forget how special it is to hear my father rumbling in the bathroom, what a small chance it is that I'll hear him clearing his throat forty years from now; even the sight of him doesn't always strike me as miraculous, as it should. All these common miracles can leave us numbed. Maybe this happens when we aren't grounded.

Well, some sons and daughters are grounded, and they do appreciate their miracles. On August 4 of this year, an eleven-year-old boy in Troy, Michigan, was hit by lightning just outside a neighbor's house. His friends had already gone inside to escape the rain. When they heard the crack of thunder, they went to the window and saw him lying on the ground beside his bicycle. Their mother raced outside and gave him mouth-to-mouth resuscitation—which she hadn't tried for fifteen years, ever since she thought maybe she'd like to be a paramedic. His grandmother said, "I just thank

God that Shelley was there to do what she did. I think God puts the right people in the right place at the right time."

As for the boy himself, although he had an enlarged left eye, a punctured eardrum, and a scar across his torso, he said, "I'm shocked, 'cause I never heard of anybody getting hit by lightning and surviving it. I'm lucky."

He got that right, and he's only eleven, going on twelve.

—ᴡᴡ—

According to Luke, right after the woman and the girl were healed, Jesus gave his twelve disciples power to heal diseases. They had some successes and failures. For the most part, chapter 9 is a record of failure. A distraught man came to Jesus about his son's epilepsy, saying, "I begged your disciples to cast it out, but they could not." Not really addressing him, Jesus burst out, "You faithless and perverse generation, how much longer must I be with you and bear with you? Bring your son here."

By contrast, consider the woman Jesus had called "daughter." Her faith, like the prayers of the righteous, had indeed been "powerful and effective." What do you suppose became of her?

Well, she could have rejoined society and, for the first time in forever, could have been with a man; she could have had a child.

Someday, though, her health must have given out and left her just as vulnerable as any of us. She had not been appointed an apostle like the Twelve, or given a gift of healing. What do you think became of her then?

And then it hits you. She had discovered the power of Jesus, and she could call upon it herself, to find peace when she really needed it. It was in her power now. She could go in peace. Her faith had made her well.

The Unqualified Christian

Sometimes you don't want to be the one to ask the question everyone is thinking. A silence fell over the disciples as Jesus told them that he would die the next day. Then he assured them that they would know the way to the place he was going. Among them were Peter, the fisherman now appointed to carry on in his name; James and John, quarreling brothers; and Matthew, a former tax collector. It's hard to imagine that any of them felt qualified to do what Jesus suggested. Thomas said, "Lord, we do not know where you are going. How can we know the way?"

A very reasonable question, in every sense of the word. It's too bad that the question mark attached itself to his name.

So many people have doubted poor Thomas. He never asked to be a model of anything for anybody—in fact he deliberately broke with his friends in saying that he would not believe their good news until he had verified it with his own eyes and hands. He was for himself, and frankly I admire this. Some have called him Doubting Thomas as if he were unqualified to join the other disciples. And yet, according to the gospel of John, the risen Christ came back especially for Thomas because he had been absent when the others had seen their Lord. When Thomas saw his hands and side and felt the wounds, he said with joy and fear and certainty, *"My Lord and my God!"* Those are the words of a disciple—that is, a Christian.

No, other Christians, and not Thomas, have hedged their bets and minced their words in ways that should rouse suspicion. I have done so myself, even as a pastor—even within this week, I am sure.

Do you know what this is? It's not a spoon or a fork: it's a spork. The food service industry has created this implement to go with any meal. Believe it or not, they give you this, without a knife, to eat a bucket of chicken.

I guess you can put it on either side of your plate. At a black-tie church picnic, it's proper for the cheese course, the fish course, the salad course, and dessert. It can spear macaroni and lift ice cream—but it can't cut. Go ahead and try.

I hate to admit how many times in my ministry I have been a spork—not too sharp, nor able to pick things up easily—a plastic pastor for simple situations. *Did Jesus rise from the dead?* Yes, but he couldn't have risen up into the skies. . . . *Is he the way for salvation?* Yes, he is for me, but salvation means something else for people of other faiths. . . . Sometimes these flexible answers just don't cut it.

—⚋⚋—

It's amazing how many folks feel they're not qualified to be Christians. They have an exalted idea of what it means to believe in Jesus.

Yes, the claims our faith makes about him are extraordinary, and it could take our whole lives to reconcile ourselves to some of them. Just the same, anyone can be his disciple—that is, his student. Look at the very first disciples, an unexceptional bunch, to say the least.

Andrew was a fisherman, not a rabbi. Simon the Zealot, a guerilla fighter. Nathanael accepted Jesus as his Lord and God so readily that even Jesus asked, "Do you believe because I told you that I saw you under the fig tree? You will see greater things than these."

Thomas didn't distinguish himself, either, until he aired his doubts, which set him apart for his honesty, I think. (As Tennyson wrote, providing a motto for Unitarians, "There lives more faith in

honest doubt/Believe me, than in half the creeds.") Thomas showed
a kind of integrity when the women said Jesus had been raised from
the dead, for his aching heart refused to traffic in pious dreams.

Most of us can identify with Thomas. We want visual, tactile,
concrete proof that the miraculous has happened, and we want it
firsthand, because we trust ourselves more than anyone else.

All that changed when Thomas saw Jesus. He touched the
scabby holes in his wrists, saw the terrible wound from the spear
in his side, heard the familiar living voice. He fell to his knees, and
never again would he trust anyone more than Jesus. He said, *"My
Lord and my God!"*

—⁂—

So are you qualified to be a Christian?

Well, let's see. You say you don't read the Bible every day.
(Hmm, that's a problem.) And you stumble over some of the
creeds. (Might not make the club.) You say you want to be a Christian even with your doubts. It might be different if you could see
him alive, with the marks in his hands and side.

But here's the real question:

Are you willing to be his disciple? To learn what Christ has to
show you, and to put it in practice?

Then you qualify. That's all it takes to be a Christian.

There are no other prerequisites. You needn't surrender every
doubt, adopt a strict diet, enter a monastery, wear a hair shirt, sleep
on nails, or occupy a pew for forty years to prove yourself worthy.
Even baptism is not necessary to be called a Christian, although it
is certainly a "sign and seal" of that relationship. The very first
people to call themselves "Christian" were a diverse community in
Antioch, and they bequeathed the name to all of us.

But here's where you and I begin to wriggle free of the gospel
responsibility—especially we mainline Christians. Because we
haven't seen the risen Christ, we sometimes have a hard time saying what we believe. We qualify our statements of faith; and say
maybe, perhaps, possibly, if . . .

Now, I don't much admire bumper-sticker declarations. But I do long for a faith as straight and true as an arrow, as uncomplicated as a heartbeat, as full of joy, fear, and certainty as Thomas's.

He was an amazing disciple. Apparently cautious by nature, he gave the first proof that he was a remarkable man by following Jesus for three years as a student and witness of wonders.

Thomas could be bluntly honest. When Jesus got word that Lazarus had died back in Bethany and decided to go there, Thomas realized immediately that it was suicide, and with black humor he said, "Let us go also, that we may die with him" (John 11:16).

After Jesus was killed, a realist such as Thomas may well have thought about going back to his old life. And yet he didn't. Apart from the Resurrection, it's hard to account for how this matter-of-fact man suddenly became heroic. No other apostle, not even Paul, traveled farther. He went to Babylon and established the first church there. Then on to Persia, and from there, India, where he won many converts. (To this day, a colony of Christians in Western India worships in Syriac, a language Thomas might have known.) Some believe that he carried the gospel as far as China before being martyred. According to tradition, he was buried in Mylapore, India.

What motivated him to travel so far, at such personal cost? I don't think it was the first three years with Jesus. No, it must have been that moment when he saw Jesus alive again, when Thomas fell to his knees and cried, *"My Lord and my God!"*

No longer a question mark, then, but an exclamation point.

—⚏—

Jesus told him, "Blessed are those who have not seen and yet believed," anticipating, perhaps, that you and I would struggle even more than Thomas. We still come to the Communion table looking for reassurance. But God help us if we ever try to feed someone else with our qualified beliefs!

There's a church not far from mine that puts on amazing retreats for pastors and their spouses. They do it just because they feel

called to do it. The last time we were there, they served a candle-
light dinner of salmon *en croûte* with crab, and a swing band
played dance music. This was a modest church in the middle of
nowhere. They just wanted us to have a first-class good time. And
the next morning those same generous laypeople would come to
lay hands on us.

That set a woman at our table to recalling with embarrassment
a reception that her church had given for new members. They didn't
know what people would like, and weren't confident enough to do
something fancy; then too, the women's society was trying to keep
it inexpensive, so they served boiled hot dogs and three-bean salad.
"And we didn't even use the church's good plates or silverware,"
she said, holding up a silver spoon beside her china cup. "The
ladies got out paper plates with sporks."

Well, at least the new members learned what they were in for.
Blessed are those churches, however, that have not seen Christ and
yet use the good silverware.

The risen Christ so changed our brother Thomas that he left his
home, then left Galilee, then left Palestine, his part of the world,
his language, left everything to share the good news with other
human beings in the farthest reaches. For the rest of his days, there
was no doubting what he was.

We have resembled him in the first chapter. Maybe we can
approach him in others, and be full-throated, unashamed, unqualified Christians who say the words: *My Lord and my God!*

Run the Race

Did you see the race? The sun shone bright on that Old Kentucky Home, bettors crowded beneath the twin spires of Churchill Downs, and for the two minutes of one of our oldest sporting spectacles, everyone had the chance to win. Yesterday was the running of the Kentucky Derby. The world's best three-year-olds were there, proud in their silks, each one eager to show the heart of a champion.

My favorite horse was not there. He was in a barn in upstate New York, biting his handlers. He has not raced since last September, and there's a reason for that. Zippy Chippy has lost more races than any thoroughbred in history.

It's not that he's without breeding; his grandsire was Northern Dancer, who certainly had the heart of a champion. But Zippy did so badly that his first owner traded him away for a battered ten-year-old van. The new owners found that Zippy bit them, kicked them, chased them out of his stall. Even the owner's wife admits that he is a "miserable, ugly-looking horse . . . poopy brown. He looks like a donkey with those ears," she says. "He's got a big butt and a little neck. He's just homely."

Good racehorses win as two- or three-year-olds. Zippy is thirteen years old, and has never won. Often he has finished dead last, and has found creative ways to lose. He has lost by a neck, and by sixty-seven lengths, and on some occasions hasn't come out of the starting gate. But he has placed second seven times, and third twelve times. "He's been losing real close," his owner declares. "He'll get it in his mind to win."

Well, maybe. He's not allowed to race in some places anymore. After Zippy lost for the eighty-fifth time, his own home track in Finger Lakes, New York, banned him "for the protection of the betting public." It wasn't a popular decision. (Believe it or not, but two horses before him had lost their first eighty-five races, and then amazingly had won number eighty-six.) But at a county fair in Massachusetts, Zippy battled hard for the first quarter mile, only to finish in the middle of the pack.

After that he lost for the eighty-seventh time, and the eighty-ninth, and the ninetieth. . .

When he was twelve, Zippy almost did the unthinkable. At one stage of the race, he opened up a five-length lead before fading to an honorable second place. Another rider lodged a protest against the winner, and if it had been upheld, Zippy would have won by default. Alas, it was denied. Zippy's owner got so excited that he entered his horse in another race the very next week—and lost for the ninety-ninth time.

That may be the end of it. Tracks everywhere have now declared him noncompetitive. I'm sorry that New York, New Jersey, and Ohio won't let Zippy persevere. He might not have a fine history, but he has the heart of a champion.

—〰—

Everybody loves a winner; everyone wants to be one. And yet success isn't a big part of the Christian story. From the very beginning of the Hebrew Bible, we have told a sacred story of human failure and discovery of the need for God.

It's surprising, but God does not call upon highly effective people, nor does God demand success. God merely asks that we do what God asks. Moses was no great speaker, yet God called on him to speak to the Israelites. Jonah hated the people of Nineveh, but God called upon him to rescue the Ninevites. And when Jeremiah, a boy in Anathoth, objected that he was just a youth, God told him to stand up straight and do the impossible—speak hard, prophetic words to his own hometown.

It might not have looked so hard at first: Anathoth was supposed
to be a city of refuge. Just the same, Jeremiah offended the people
so deeply that they tried to kill him. Small wonder that he complained to God about this impossible assignment. (He was a good
complainer. Check out the Book of Lamentations.) God gently
chided him, "If you have raced with foot-runners and they have
wearied you, how will you compete with horses? And if in a safe
land you fall down, how will you fare in the thickets of the Jordan?" Even as Jeremiah's own family turned against him, God still
expected the boy to prophesy and be a faithful spokesman.

Which he did. Which is why his name has lasted for a hundred
generations.

Our secular world demands success, but God asks only faith-
fulness. Results matter almost nothing to God, merely our actions.
As the Psalmist says:

> His delight is not in the strength of the horse,
>   nor his pleasure in the speed of a runner;
> but the LORD takes pleasure in those who fear him,
>   in those who hope in his steadfast love.
>
> (Ps. 147:10–11)

Do we have such faith? I am afraid that we lose heart over small
things. And let's be honest—Christianity requires stamina, relent-
less honesty with oneself and with God, and acceptance of each
day's trials.

Some people, especially those who thought God would make
their lives easier, drop out right away. Others give up because so-
called Christian behavior doesn't come naturally to them: it's hard
for them not to judge or be angry, or to do away with pride, or to
trust God, so they tell themselves they must not be cut out for this,
as if anybody is.

Look, no one has been bred for this. No one is a Christian simply by virtue of parentage. Bloodline has nothing to do with it. We
all are entered merely by the grace of Jesus Christ, grace that
applies to us equally, because, God knows, we all need it.

—᳁—

For more than thirty years, Ernest Fremont Tittle preached to the First Methodist Church of Evanston, Illinois. Tittle was a progressive preacher—a staunch pacifist and integrationist—in a deeply Republican suburb where ladies lunched. Local gossip had it that he actually played ball on Sundays with his boys behind the parsonage.

He scandalized some people when he published a book called *What Must the Church Do to Be Saved?* Just the same, crowds turned out to hear what he had to say. During his long, productive tenure, the congregation doubled.

In the Red scare days of the 1930s, a local chapter of the American Legion called him a Communist. The *Chicago Tribune* and both Hearst newspapers in Chicago took up the cry and campaigned for him to be thrown out of his pulpit. Tittle, a veteran of the First World War, figured his congregation knew him better than that. But as he faced a daily assault in print, longtime members and friends began to doubt him and melt away.

Tittle began to feel pains in his chest. Still they didn't keep him from causes he felt to be right. He proposed that the Methodist General Conference hold its meetings only in cities where Negro delegates could eat and sleep as freely as whites. Now he was not only a dangerous Red, he was a "nigger lover."

The hue and cry grew tremendous until at last, in a moment of historic courage, his church board issued a public statement of support, declaring that they stood for a free pulpit and a free church, effectively ending the clamor.

Somehow Tittle kept his humor, even in days that seemed to call for a jeremiad. Years later, he may have had a wry smile on his face as he told this story:

Once there was a young man in Anathoth, a small town not far from Jerusalem, who was called of God to be a preacher. He began his ministry in his home town and was not well received. Quite the contrary. A group of influential people, taking umbrage at the things he was saying, determined to get rid of him. In fact, they even went so far as to plot against his life. When the young preacher learned of this, not unnaturally he was upset. In his anxiety he turned to God for some word of encouragement, and the word that came was this: "If you have run with men on foot, and they have tired you out, then how will you keep up with horses?"

"Strange comfort!" observed Tittle. "Like the whimsical admonition, 'Cheer up, the worst is yet to come.' Yet in Jeremiah's case it availed. Life for him did become more strenuous, more difficult and dangerous. But learning to run with men on foot and not get all tired out, he won the power to keep up with horses."[11]

—⁓—

Over against the American ideal of success, which is to impress and surpass the neighbors, is the Christian virtue of perseverance. The greatest failure of all belonged to Jesus. For three years he was the talk of Palestine. A peaceable army followed him into Jerusalem as crowds waved palm braches and acclaimed him as a king. He was supposed to redeem his country, restore the line of David to the throne in Israel, and inaugurate a reign of peace. It didn't happen. To the crushing disappointment of his followers, he submitted mildly to arrest, went without a fight to his death, crowned with thorns and mocked as a cautionary "King of the Jews." The earthly powers had their say. He looked like an utter failure.

The cross could be a symbol of failure. But it is not. There has never been a success like his.

To this day, he calls us to perseverance: "No one who puts a hand to the plow and looks back is fit for the kingdom of God." "Not everyone who cries, Lord, Lord, will be saved." "Are you able to drink the cup that I drink?" By ordinary business standards, the church isn't very successful—ninety-seven, ninety-eight, ninety-nine times in a row we fail to get the message out. Yet somehow we endure.

The Kentucky Derby is not a distance race, only a mile and a quarter. It's over in about two minutes. For the long distance that we must run, God has said, "A new heart I will give you," and you know whose it is. It is the heart of a champion.

Old News

*T*he big presses roll, the paper rolls in sheets; suddenly pages appear with pictures and headlines, and before the gigantic machine is done these pages are cut, folded, and bundled. From here, a schoolchild with a bicycle and basket can take the lesson: there's money to be made in selling news.

But only while it's new. The Sunday paper goes for a buck and a half; this newspaper from Friday is sold for fifty cents, and what's it worth today? Maybe the paper it's printed on.

It's a strange afterlife, what happens to old news.

Once magazines expire, my local newsstand sends most of them right back to a distributor, while others, minus their covers, go to charity. The library keeps magazines on the shelves for three years, when they're offered to the public for free, and any left unclaimed get pitched.

Newspapers suffer greater indignities; hardly anybody wants old newspapers. Libraries don't want them—in fact, libraries have been tossing out their bound volumes of historic newspapers dating back over a hundred years because they just don't have the space. A business in New Jersey sells copies of big-city papers as birthday gifts, but has no use for small-town papers like mine. No, unsold copies of those papers will be shredded into insulation, or loaded onto a semi and taken in a few months to the city dump.

Joy, grief, births, deaths, politics and comic strips and wedding announcements—that's where they go, and nobody seems to mind, because more is coming tomorrow, for another fifty cents.

Now that many of us get our news online, where stories come and go at the speed of light, it is downright sobering to think what happens to news. Even where stories are archived, you'll only find what you're looking for; you may never happen upon something delightful by mere chance as you did formerly by slowly turning the pages of a bound collection. Quirky stories, always quick to fade, will vanish into the ether.

But there is some very old news that refuses to go gently into that good night. It comes to us personally, persistently, and indeed it seems to be about us: those are our stories, our pictures in the ancient pages. Our accidents, our secrets are told there, and so too are family histories and quiet blessings that no one else could know. And then, very curiously, there are accounts of decisions we might make, changes that may someday take place within us. Most news is instantly old, but this has never aged: in fact it has come from tomorrow. It tells us what we haven't seen yet.

—∿∿—

Here is a man who worked in a small city stitching tents and studying his religion with the fire of youth. What he ate, what he wore, what he read, to whom he spoke, all mattered to him intensely.

When an equally fanatic young man from a splinter sect dared to challenge those received ideas and the proud history of their shared faith, the first young man held coats for the mob as they gathered stones and killed his counterpart. Perhaps he was chagrined not to have thrown stones himself, for he signed up as a vigilante, and was hot on the trail of other heretics when he was struck down on the Damascus Road.

This was where the story changed. Up to this point, young Saul had lived in the Old Testament. From then on, he lived in the New Testament. In fact, he *wrote* much of the New Testament—literally: his response to the gospel eclipsed even the output of Matthew, Mark, or John. The gospel had come to him personally, and although it was first and foremost about Jesus of Nazareth, it was also about him. It changed everything about him, even his name: for its sake, he took the name Paul, from the Greek word for "little." He never repudiated his past, as cultists do, but cherished it as the seed of his new being. Perhaps the best expression of this was how this devout Jew enlisted as a missionary to the Gentiles and risked his life for them. All of this was because the good news had come to him personally.

Now, it needs to be said that the Christian designation of Old and New Testaments doesn't really do justice to Judaism, and is inherently offensive. Even Jesus himself, who didn't mind offending people, might have blanched at such terms. He said that he had come "not to overthrow, but to fulfill" the law, and if his message was like heady new wine, he could understand that for most folks the mellow, mature wine went down a lot better. Those of us who have admired the good news have often clipped it from its roots, stuck it in a vase, and watched it die.

The truth is that Old and New are simultaneous, and happen in concert, forever giving each other life and relevance. The Old is still happening in the New, and both are still happening in us.

—◊◊◊—

Whatever changed Paul wound up changing the life of his young protégé Timothy. We don't know that Timothy's name changed, but we do learn from Paul's surviving letters to Timothy some of what passed between them. Early in the first letter, Paul alludes to his own story:

> I am grateful to Christ Jesus our Lord, who has strengthened me, because he judged me faithful and appointed me to his service, even though I was formerly a blasphemer, a persecutor, and a man of violence. But I received mercy because I had acted ignorantly in unbelief, and the grace of our Lord overflowed for me with the faith and love that are in Christ Jesus. The saying is sure and worthy of full acceptance, that Christ Jesus came into the world to save sinners—of whom I am the foremost. (1 Timothy 1:12–15)

Paul's former life is very much present in this letter. If he has any authority, it is not as an apostle, but as "the foremost of sinners."

Which leads him to a modest, tender way of encouraging Timothy, his spiritual son and heir:

> I am giving you these instructions, Timothy, my child, in accordance with the prophecies made earlier about you, so that by following them you may fight the good fight, having faith and a good conscience. (1 Timothy 1:18–19)

2×

Now this is a passage we don't often hear. Prophecies made about Timothy? When and what were those? Did someone say something about Timothy? Did angels announce his coming? Was he born of a virgin and laid in a manger? No—but the past was present in him, through his grandmother Lois and mother Eunice, Jewish women who had become followers of this New Way. Paul writes:

> I am grateful to God—whom I worship with a clear conscience, as my ancestors did—when I remember you constantly in my prayers night and day. . . . I am reminded of your sincere faith, a faith that lived first in your grandmother Lois and your mother Eunice and now, I am sure, lives in you. (2 Timothy 1:3, 5)

I'm just guessing that Lois and Eunice made those prophecies about him. They may have seen that his mixed parentage (Jewish mother, Greek father) made him useful to Paul. Certainly he offered Paul a proof of his faith by undergoing circumcision to reassure the Jews they met. (Apparently Paul had changed so much that he needed Timothy to vouch for his commitment to the Old Covenant.) With his terrible past as the foremost of sinners always before him, Paul brought Timothy into a completely new life.

And what a life it must have been for this young man, picked up and taken out of sleepy Lystra into a whirlwind of travels. Although new things must have been happening within him all the time, we have no record of them—no letter *from* Timothy, no journal, no jotting from his bedside late at night, nothing to indicate his inner life. All we know is that he grew up in a hurry. Paul urged him to stay in Ephesus, a dangerous spot indeed, and according to tradition Timothy became bishop there. That's about all that we know, except for the most important thing—that the prophecy was fulfilled in a chain of believers, stretching all the way to this week.

—ᴦᴎᴧ—

When Paul wrote to Timothy, he could not have expected his letters to survive, and it's very unlikely that he had us in mind. But sometimes, by the grace of God, human words have divine life, which is what makes scripture different from, say, the *Times-Indicator.* And sure enough, those words have sought me out.

Here I am on a Thursday morning, bolting down a bran muffin and reading that first letter to Timothy because it's expected for a sermon. These have been some painful days lately in the congregation. It just so happens that my tired eye falls on these words, which may not be for anybody else but me personally: "Let no one despise your youth, but set the believers an example in speech and conduct, in love, in faith, in purity. . . . Do not neglect the gift that is in you, which was given to you through prophecy with the laying on of hands by the council of elders."

Good morning.

The whole idea of a newspaper fosters an addiction as powerful as caffeine—that we can take refuge in vicarious thrills, tragedies, sweeping causes instead of what God has poured into our own cup. Each newspaper takes the life of the one before it because the illusion is so fragile. Scripture, on the other hand, waits patiently to give us a personal prophecy.

Who are we, really? And what are we supposed to do with our lives? That's what God wants us to discover.

Emerson said, "A man gets acquainted with himself, but is always a surprise. We get news daily of the world within, as well as the world outside, and not less of the central than of the surface facts. A new thought is waiting him every morning." Of course, by now the gospel should be old news. We have heard the story so many times now, we should have wadded it up. On any given day, however, it can hit us as if for the first time. We are spectators to most of the news we get, but this good news involves us personally. We find pieces of it playing out in our own lives. It tells us who we will become.

Everything Must Go

*H*ere in the rural upper Midwest, it seems every other person has a pole barn. Usually it's full of old tires, old brakes, a trailer, dozens of tools gathering rust, coffee cans loaded with lug nuts and screws. But then almost nobody in America lives like the desert monks.

Ed and Edna's place is pretty typical, I think. Her cupboards, bureaus, cabinets, garage, attic, and spare bedroom have been crammed full of things that define her. ("Oh, you know Edna Furbelow," says her neighbor, "she collected Hummels.") Every once in a while, she took some of the clutter out to the front yard and sold it, although no one stepping inside her house ever knew the difference. Now that Edna has died and her husband's pole barn has finally gotten emptied, everything must go.

It's too bad she's not here for the lesson, because there's something morally instructive about an estate sale. Absent the owners, the items lose their meaning, so that even Ed and Edna's kids and closest friends think, *My God, there's a lot of stuff here. What a lot of junk!* The agent, who doesn't want to haul it away, has priced everything low: books go for fifty cents, a big set of plates for a few bucks. Here is an old rusty bicycle from the Eisenhower era and a once-prized lamp that now seems hideous. Set out on the green grass outside the barn, Ed's band saw and drill press, his pride and joy, appear headed for retirement.

Now the auctioneer calls out Lot 152, a collection of four hundred Hummels. Eyes roll and knowing smiles break out, but no one bids. The auctioneer looks at the estate agent, the agent looks at Edna's oldest daughter: a lifetime's hobby and a person's identity have come to this. It's almost possible to hear Jesus asking, *And these Hummels, whose will they be?*

To everything there is a season, of course, yet these days it seems to me that the most profound book of the Bible is Ecclesiastes. Here are no promises about the beyond—only a dead-level gaze and a calm voice saying, "You are mortal." We have distracted ourselves with so many pleasures and ambitions, to which the Preacher says, The pleasures are fine, but the ambitions are futile.

Who was this Ecclesiastes? Tradition sometimes says Solomon, though he doesn't sound like Solomon, not by a long shot. He doesn't sound like a preacher, either. He's a poet of world-weariness, an absurdist and existentialist three thousand years before the smart alecks, a man of faith and no faith, none, not a drop, in human doings. All we do is vanity, illusory, impermanent, and his faith, such as it is, begins with that erasure. When you come face to face with that, then you can no longer be the god of your own life. You have killed the biggest idol that there is. Not many people do that.

Ecclesiastes declared himself weary of everything littering his garage and driveway—RVs, snowmobiles, hobby cars. For Jesus it must have been simpler. All he left behind was a cloak (still serviceable) and his mother. And that's how he truly left the world as naked as he came in.

But in another sense, Jesus left behind so much more. The poor of his day knew grinding poverty and powerlessness. And he gave up everything to be with them. The Christ hymn of Philippians, perhaps the oldest Christian text surviving, makes this stunning acclamation:

> Though he was in the form of God, [he] did not count equality with God a thing to be grasped, but emptied himself, taking the form of a servant, being born in the likeness of men. And being found in human form he humbled himself and became obedient unto death, even death on a cross.
>
> Therefore God has highly exalted him and bestowed on him the name which is above every name, that at the name of Jesus

every knee should bow, in heaven and on earth and under the earth, and every tongue confess that Jesus Christ is Lord, to the glory of God the Father. (Philippians 2:6–11)

He gave up a normal human life. He gave up all the privileges and power of divinity. He didn't seem to give up much, but the broken pieces of what he left behind were more than enough to fill twelve baskets.

—⚊—

Which brings us to Jesus's story about the man who stored up grain for many seasons in his barns, with such a surplus that he thought of building bigger barns. I don't know, maybe they were pole barns.

> "The land of a rich man produced abundantly. And he thought to himself, 'What should I do, for I have no place to store my crops?' Then he said, 'I will do this: I will pull down my barns and build larger ones, and there I will store all my grain and my goods. And I will say to my soul, Soul, you have ample goods laid up for many years; relax, eat, drink, be merry.' But God said to him, 'You fool! This very night your life is being demanded of you. And the things you have prepared, whose will they be?' " (Luke 12:16–20)

This parable is a burlesque of Ecclesiastes 9:7 ("Go, eat your bread with enjoyment, and drink your wine with a merry heart; for God has long ago approved what you do"). Say what you will about him, the rich man is a sort of philosopher. Life has provided him an early retirement, and rather than waste his time working for more, he's going to rest and enjoy himself. His motto could be *carpe diem*. To a lot of us, he would seem a healthy and balanced sort of guy, but he has left no grain for the gleaners, the widows and the orphans, and the only tithe he has offered is a sigh of contentment.

In the end, this story is about other people, the poor, who would have gleaned from his fields. It is also about Jesus himself, the wealthy man who gave up everything to be with them. And even though this parable squarely faces mortality, it's not jaded or hope-less—far from it. If you hold it up to a mirror, as you should with all parables, the reverse image offers hope of an everlasting life.

Altogether, it's a much more profound story than Ecclesiastes would have told. Come to think of it, the most profound voice in the Bible just may be Jesus's.

—⟋⟍⟍⟋—

In the name of this Christ, we get so many things wrong. A few years ago you heard lots of talk about the antichrist. The year 2000, which meant nothing to the Bible writers, was coming, and some rural Christians expected a catastrophe. All the computers in the world were supposed to crash, and global chaos would ensue. Pas-tors advised their flocks to stock shelters with rice and beans, portable generators, and ammunition. Never mind that this fear was totally at odds with the gospel, which promises that God looks after the sparrows and the lilies of the field no less than his own children. Never mind that hoarding food supplies and guarding these supplies with guns was totally at odds with the gospel. No, if that time was notable for anything, it was that Christians them-selves had become anti-Christians.

In late September of 2001, folks started bringing some of these groceries to local food pantries, and at last these survival items went to people who needed them to survive. Needy folks gleaned what they could of powdered milk, powdered eggs, canned fruit.

Jesus is still telling stories about us, stories too good to keep.

Not too far from Ed and Edna's place, two young parents are trying to make a go of it in a trailer on her folks' property. Family obligations and the threat of financial ruin hang over them con-stantly and strain their marriage. She was working at Wal-Mart until the second baby came along; now they have to hunt for the very lowest bargains. So they are here at the estate sale, picking through the tables, gleaning what they can.

"Everything must go," says the sign over the children's clothes. They date back to the 1970s, amazingly preserved in tissue by

Edna for her grandchildren, never imagining whose hands would take them now.

Well, isn't it about time? Everything belongs to God, so everything must go for a good cause. And if we have not been generous in our lifetimes, God will compel us to give those things away, for someday we must go, too.

Taste Test

"*I* have become all things to all people," Paul wrote to the Corinthians, apparently not foreseeing how we would regard his wry boast. Today his efforts to ingratiate himself with very different people sound inauthentic, phony—and impossible. "You can't be all things to all people," is how one of my seminary professors put it. And it was a Methodist seminary.

But Paul, the devout Jew who remarkably became a missionary to the Gentiles, didn't see it that way. As he met Gentiles and sampled their customs, their food, their drink, he remained entirely himself. More himself than ever. Peter, too, delicately refused to try the crawfish and andouille sausage until he had that dream about unclean animals being brought down from heaven on a table-cloth, and then he knew that it was okay to eat with the Gentiles, that he could sit down with them and still be Peter, a very Jewish Christian. "The Spirit told me to go with them and not to make a distinction between them and us," he said.

Just like Jesus, who was completely himself even in the company of sinners, Peter and Paul took on some of the qualities of those they served. Evangelism, it turns out, is a two-way street.

A real relationship changes you. Unfortunately we Christians often manifest a desire to reach all people without a willingness to "become all things" in the process. We want folks to "taste and see that the LORD is good," while they want us to taste what *they* have and find out who they are.

87

At bitter Valley Forge, amid the hunger and low morale, George Washington was on his rounds trying to bolster the men when he came upon some of them drinking. Private John Brantley invited him to "drink some wine with a soldier." General Washington said, "My boy, you have no time for drinking wine," and started to go on his way.

Private Brantley cried, "Damn your proud soul! You're above drinking with soldiers."

Washington said, "Come, I will drink with you," and took a pull from the jug.

Brantley recklessly told him to give it next to his "servants," who were in fact officers. Washington did so.

When they were done, so the story goes, Private Brantley took it and said, "Now, *I'll* be damned if I don't spill the last drop of my heart's blood for you."

—ᴡ—

To readers of Paul's letters, the church at Corinth sounds like a pretty rough place. The people there were arguing, roistering, pretty much making up for themselves how they would take the Lord's Supper. Apparently some of them came hungry for a lot of bread or to get drunk. Paul was rightly horrified that anyone should take Christ's body and blood so casually. So in a manner of speaking, he gave them lessons in etiquette.

Bear in mind that Paul was writing maybe twenty-five or thirty years at most after Jesus's death. He reminded the people of Corinth how Jesus had taken bread and broken it, taken the cup and blessed it, and given them to his disciples. Paul didn't use the word *sacrament;* it doesn't appear in the Bible. Such a word would have seemed to him too symbolic for Christ's body and blood. To regard them as mere bread and wine was to invite abuses, which Paul found personally embarrassing after having fought to include these Gentiles in the church.

"Whoever, then, eats the body or drinks the cup of the Lord in an unworthy manner," he said, "will be answerable for the body and the blood of the Lord." That's what the Jerusalem church was worried about—that if Paul let Gentiles into the church, they might still be themselves.

Yes, yes, we must approach the sacrament with reverence. And yet the meal was first given to disciples who didn't understand it and had just been jockeying for position at the table. The very word *sacrament* means mystery, which means it is bound to be handled roughly, without comprehension. Even today, we don't understand it all that well. It is an invitation I don't fully understand, although it becomes clearer when squirrelly third-graders hang around after the service and ask if they can have the leftover bread and juice. They're just being themselves.

—✺—

New pastors like to imagine that they're easily approachable. Tempted to prove that we are still worldly, we may cuss and smoke and generally try hard to be "ordinary" until at last we realize that we are still pastors. But far more often, I think, the Gentiles have to coax us out of false pieties and insist that we meet them in their world.

Fresh out of seminary, assigned to my first church, I met all sorts of interesting characters who on Sunday mornings dressed in Sunday clothes and wore Sunday expressions on their faces, but come Monday were gloriously themselves again.

Bud and Amber Shirah, for example, were in their middle sixties. A more conventional country couple you never saw. He still had the gait of someone who rode horses, while she was all round, with a big round sweet face, and baked pies and sang softly in the choir. After one Sunday service, they filed out with the crowd, and Bud said to me, "Like to get to know you. Have you over sometime. How about this week?"

I said sure, and went out to their place a few days later. At first I thought I'd turned down the wrong drive. A motorcycle came tearing up beside me; a fat man all in black leather screeched to a stop and took off his helmet. I could just barely tell that behind the tinted sunglasses was Bud. Bud?

Bud said, "Bet you never knew you had a hog in the church, did you? How's that grab you?" It was just fine, and when I asked about his machine, he proudly described it in detail, showed me his garage, where parts and pans and plugs lay all around. Over by the workbench was a picture of silver-haired Amber, in her riding gear.

She came on out and said hello in that sweet choir voice. I asked, "Why don't you ride your bikes over to church sometime?" "Well, we just might, if you keep talking like that," she said. "Be careful what you wish for."

"No, honey, no," Bud said, "we've got to be respectable people now. We've found the Lord. We don't want to shock those fine, upstanding people by arriving that way. They might have a committee meeting about it." Then he said, "I bet you're thirsty. Let's go inside, and I'll have you try something."

A breeze blew through their small house. Bud went into the kitchen and brought out two small wineglasses and a bottle of his own wine, made just that summer. "Bud," I said, "it's ten-thirty in the morning." "That just means the day's a-wasting," he said, and poured me a glass.

Now, you can file what happened next under peer pressure or pastoral ministry. That first glass of wine went down like paint thinner. Bud poured other varieties of grape, and they had not mellowed either. Over the next hour we tried raspberry, blackberry, elderberry, cherry, black currant, and dandelion wine. He kept asking how I liked them. What could I say, except, "This is a first for me"?

"You're a different sort of Methodist preacher," he said, in what I hoped was a compliment.

At last he poured a thick glass of something dark red. "This is my favorite. Not everybody goes for this," he said.

The bouquet—no, the smell—was indescribable. It was like old lawn clippings and gasoline and a V-8 cocktail. "That's tomato wine," he said. "Go ahead."

If I live to be ninety, I'll still choke at the thought of it. But by the time it reached my gullet, I was all things to all people and had entered Bud's circle.

It was just past noon, and my workday was done. My head was spinning from how Bud had sized me up and decided he could trust me, and from that time on we had quite a relationship.

Every day, ministry offers the privilege of becoming all things to all people; and I have never been more myself.

Labors of Love

I would rather do anything else; there is nothing I would rather do. Today I am heading out to see Alma, a widowed former school-teacher, now confined to the ground floor of her home by asthma and poor vision. Seeing her this afternoon means I have had to cut short a phone call from an old friend. Two hundred and fifty years ago, Samuel Johnson groused, "I hate to meet John Wesley. The dog enchants with his conversation, and then breaks away to go and visit some old woman."

How did I get into this, anyway? Whose bright idea was it to put a questioning English major in a Saturn sedan, turning down this gravel road? It sure wasn't mine—not till I was twenty-one; not till an elderly college professor took me under his wing and offered Sunday meals if I would join him and his wife for church. It was his idea that I might be a pastor, or maybe it was someone else's.

In the rear-view mirror all I can see is a plume of dust.

The siding on Alma's house has not been painted in years, and the concrete steps have sunk into the grass, leaving one long step that she probably doesn't attempt anymore. She doesn't come to the door anymore—visitors just go in. She's not helpless, however; the meals she has cooked are still on the table and in the sink. And even though her conversation is often pieced together from memory and confusion, Alma can be very sharp. "Thank goodness my television has only three channels," she says. "If I had cable I might never again have an original thought."

A cat comes in with a few cousins.

"Are those cats in here again? Just tell them to stay here and they'll go right back out to the yard."

Maybe forty cats have established command and control of the grounds, giving the house an overpowering aroma of urine and fur. No wonder she has asthma—a person can hardly breathe. Fortunately Alma can't see me wiping my nose as two longhaired Persians nuzzle and paw my leg.

She offers me some cookies from the kitchen, if I want to get them. On the way I pass some pictures of her in her vital years—of her travels with friends; of her late husband. Over time, she has become ever more herself, wise, conversant, with her own sharp takes on politics. Still the schoolteacher, she has high standards for clear thinking and expression, high standards for herself. Alma asks me if she's getting crotchety. "I live by the Eleventh Commandment," she declares: "Thou shalt not be the last straw." It's true that her personality has been brewed so long that it's very strong, with no cream, no sugar.

Late in the afternoon, in the darkening parlor, we finally get around to discussing the things that weigh on her the most. "I have been having a hard time managing out here," she sighs.

Her son has kept her books for years, and has checked in occasionally, but lately he has been gone for months at a time, leaving her high and dry. Bills have been piling up and collection agencies have begun to call. She's worried that she could lose her savings.

Just by coming out here today, I have stumbled on this matter that she has confided to no one else yet. It's hard to say why she has chosen to talk about it now. I certainly can't inspire confidence, and yet somehow we cover important ground. We talk about dealing with her son, about maybe having a friend from the bank set up some direct payments. We talk about her recent falls and other medical emergencies, about her isolation from remaining friends. Does she really want to stay in this house? She does. Her voice rises with emphasis: she does. This is not unlike working things out with an aged parent or grandparent, and it's impossible to feel anything but love.

By now the shadows are so deep that she needs to switch on a lamp—which is my cue to go home. Before I go, we share a prayer. We've done this before, so she knows that she can give it. It pleases her to put her problems in words for God.

"Almighty God," she says, "unto whom all hearts are open, all desires known, and from whom no secrets are hid . . ." When we finish, her bright eyes acknowledge that she has been teaching again. She has spent a few hours turning an uncertain young man into her pastor.

—⟋⟍⟍—

The apostle Paul had a multiple-point circuit way out in the country, where the district superintendent had sent him to preach to the Gentiles. He wouldn't have called it exactly a career choice—it had chosen him. Before taking up the call, he had been a tent-maker—and still was, in more ways than ever.

He loved it, loved the people. You hear it in his letters. Here is the First Letter to the Thessalonians: *We always give thanks to God for all of you and mention you in our prayers, constantly remembering before our God and Father your work of faith and labor of love . . .*

And yet it wasn't easy for him; folks said he was unimpressive, a poor talker, a disappointment after that striking young man Apollos.

What Paul had going for him was conviction born out of an intensely personal vision—that Jesus, whose followers he had persecuted, loved him anyway. An explosion of reality had made all the other conditions of life seem less real. It was as if a depth charge had gone off and floated fish to the surface. Most of the folks he spoke to had heard something about Jesus; he had come in their lifetimes, in their part of the world. Some of them had even seen Jesus. They all had met religious people before, but Paul was not talking about a myth from long ago—what he was talking about was immediate, and called for an immediate personal response. He was talking about love.

—∽∿∽—

There are so many things to be done. On Tuesday, the start of the week, several pastors get together for breakfast and talk about the pastors who aren't there. They hear old Rick is really taking a beating over at his place. Back at my office, there's mail to sort through, phone calls to return, and a restless retiree who drops by frequently just to chat. People in the hospital need a visit; housebound members would like me to bring Communion. Mid-afternoon, my secretary reaches me on the road to say that the furnace inspector has finally arrived. The workday continues well into the night, with appearances at a Boy Scout dinner and a meeting of the missions committee. On Wednesday, there's the men's breakfast at the coffee shop, and right after that the staff meeting, the worship planning meeting, a counseling session, and just after lunch a drawn-out brainstorming session for Christian education. Even though none of this got taught at seminary, it has become the shape of ministry. And then there's Robbie.

Robbie wore out her welcome at the social service agencies a long time ago, and on a couple of occasions has taken our church for a ride. Her poverty is real, no doubt; I've seen the places where she lives. But she lives a hard life, and runs through help like water, and after a while you want to tell her enough's enough.

This week she has called the church over and over to ask for groceries. When she calls again today, I invite her to come to the food pantry on Monday. She says she doesn't have a car. Couldn't someone drive some food out her way? "I haven't had nothing to eat in four days," she moans.

Folks who come to the pantry usually take whatever we have. Robbie wants smoked turkey, lean roast beef, and a pound of coffee, but it has to be decaf.

A bad storm has dumped a foot of snow. Unwilling to saddle someone else with this chore, I trudge down to the food pantry, fill a few grocery sacks, and drive the twenty miles out to her latest place, now and then muttering under my breath. The apartment is as awful as one can imagine: a single-story cinder-block building with a rotted roof. No one has bothered to plow the lot.

Robbie can see me coming. She steps out of her door, smoking a cigarette. "Did you bring me the coffee?" she asks. "Decaf?"

I stop about twenty yards out from her door. The snow is just so thick.

"Pastor," she says, "could you pull up a little closer?"

"Robbie, just stay there," I say, and wade through the drifts with first one sack, then the other, feeling the burden in my lower back.

She fairly beams. And before a conversation can begin, I say, "Well, I think that's about it," and leave without asking anything about her or what more she might need. It is not one of my better days in ministry.

I do, however, feel lighter, in more ways than one. Despite myself, I feel glad to have been of some help. And about a hundred yards down the road, I have the odd feeling that when I am judged, it will be by what I do for Robbie.

Although Paul could recount truly heroic labors, he seemed proudest that he and his churches had built mutual affection. He listed extraordinary spiritual gifts a Christian might have, but the greatest of these, he said, was love. In fact, he was so overwhelmed by the love shown to him by the risen Christ, and by the people of Ephesus, who would have plucked out their eyes and given them to him, that he had no choice in the matter: he was "compelled to preach the gospel."

Surely there were days when he would have wanted to do anything else. We all have dreams of escape, breaking free of our bonds, just as children might lie on the grass and dream of falling up into the bowl of the sky. If only, by the power of mind, they could do it! But the earth holds them fast, of course.

Something like that force rules us and holds us fast despite every effort (mostly of the imagination) to escape. A small body is attracted to something larger than itself; we could say that this gravitational force is Newtonian, although the Newton would not be Isaac but John, the slave trader who came to tears and a discovery of amazing grace.

We are drawn to this immensity just as surely as apples fall to the grass. It is futile to pretend that we are not. As the great saint Augustine said about all bodies in motion, "Thou hast made us for thyself, and our hearts are restless until they find rest in thee."

The question that daily perplexes pastors is whether this means we must serve a church. The idea of anything else can be appealing—running a bed and breakfast, say, or teaching high school. Something normal. Something else. Plenty of colleagues have bailed out; some have found the hoped-for normal life.

And some have found very valid ministries beyond the church. A most eloquent refugee, Barbara Brown Taylor, admits, "I miss leading worship, I miss baptisms, and I miss funerals, and I miss hospital calls, and I miss nursing homes. I really miss that a lot. But I think my dream would be to find a group of people who would sign on the dotted line that they intend never to become an institution. I'd go back for that, but I wouldn't take pay. I hope I would never take pay again to do that 'cause it felt too much like being paid to love. And you know what that is, when you get paid to love."[12]

Well, maybe that's a little unfair: the prostitute isn't paid to love, but to fake love—or to make no pretense of love at all. You wouldn't say the same thing about a nurse.

But then again, Barbara Brown Taylor may be right after all. Sometimes the nurse and the pastor have to fake love; the feeling isn't always there.

And yet . . . if the apostle Paul had to fake his affection for troubled churches, his letters sure don't sound like it. Rather they resonate with real kinship, in spite of all. He was not a patient man by nature. He had to become one because of his calling. God used his passionate nature, even tears and anger sometimes, to emphasize the reality of his love. The borrowed beds, the begged meals, the rides he cadged on freighters bound for distant cities, took the sharp edge off his pride and made him grateful for other people. He could name them: Lydia, Prisca, Aquila, Onesimus, Erastus,

Titus, Tychicus, Epaphras, Luke, Robbie. Thanks to what he learned through them, this unnatural life became second nature.

Jesus said, "My yoke is easy, and my burden is light." Love is the lightest of responsibilities. What else do we mean by a labor of love? The difficulty for us is when we take up the labor before the love. When we get it right, the work of love is hardly work at all.

—ᴍ—

Two days before our church conference with the district superintendent, my secretary is taking apart a balky photocopier, coaxing it to print a few more booklets. Both phone lines ring; she asks me to step over piles of papers to answer them. At that moment, the restless retiree appears, just hanging in the doorframe, and observes that we look busy. Maybe he should come back another time.

Maybe I should agree, but instead I motion for him to stay. Patiently waiting for our attention, stuffing his hands in his pockets, he mills about, then seizes the moment when the phone calls are done to ask after our families, plainly wanting us to ask about his. It turns out that his niece has just been diagnosed with leukemia. He talks about it matter-of-factly at first, but we seem to be drifting toward my office. Eventually, behind the closed door, he shares a curious story.

When he was in the Navy, he met an ensign from Wichita, of all places, a kid with huge feet and a funny voice, who became his closest friend. Two Midwestern kids way out in the Pacific, rolling all over the deck. Well, by the time their ship reached Inchon, most of the guys had come down with something or other, and this friend of his never caught a thing. Other guys got hurt or killed, and he never caught a bullet. The kid from Wichita got him reading the Bible, and that's where he became a Christian, way out there. Then after the war this other kid went home to Kansas, not a bit of water for him to drown in, and came down with leukemia.

We sit in silence for a while.

I give him a hug and ask him to tell me about his niece.

She sounds like a spirited young woman, a volleyball player. Of course, cancer treatments have improved greatly since his friend died, but he's not at all sure what they can do for her. And anyway, he has other kinds of questions. He admits to be being mad at God. We talk a little about our own mortality, which is really the issue. For all his faith, he still has mixed feelings about dying. He says he's had a full life, but when I ask if maybe he has an even fuller one ahead of him, he gives me a quizzical look. That's what he really wants to know, he says. It's getting time.

He also wants to do something for his niece, so we join hands and pray, and speaking to God again seems to help him. As we finish, it occurs to me that he still needs something else to do. Would he like to help out around the office now and then? He smiles, a very capable and transparent man. Why, yes, he'd be glad to fold bulletins, sharpen pencils for the sanctuary, whatever. By the time he takes his leave, neither of us feels quite so helpless.

Some time later there is a knock at my office door, and in walks a bald man in a very plain blue suit and a solid blue tie; he even has a blue vein across his forehead. Wearing a fixed smile, he asks, "Lawrence? Do you have a moment?" This is a bad signal: everybody around here calls me Larry.

Still, he seems intent, and the day has shown you never know what burden the poor guy might be carrying. I invite him to sit down.

Actually, he tells me, he is a pastor himself. He has served a Lutheran church not too far away for almost twenty years. He lights up at the sight of books on my shelf and tells a little story of how Emil Brunner went down with the country folk at his first parish. As he describes the place he serves today, I feel a kinship with him and a shared pride in what we do. "People fascinate me," he says, "finding out what their needs are, and helping them to make decisions.

"That's why I started selling life insurance. Lawrence, do you have a family?"

Nonplussed, I admit that I do.

"Do you have coverage?"

Well . . . yes. A small policy.

"A starter policy. Not enough to put kids through college, eh?"

He reaches into his portfolio. "Things have changed since you had a child." By now the smile has vanished.

Describing at some length the company he represents, and using my given name again, he goes on, "Lawrence, let me tell you what we can provide you. We offer term coverage, with which you're familiar, I'm sure. And whole life—a good investment that you can borrow against. A lot of people like whole life because it's a disciplined way to provide for your future. What I'd recommend to most young families like yours is that you consider universal coverage . . ."

I have never really considered before all the similarities between pastors and insurance salesmen. Suddenly the idea of another career takes on a startling reality: here is the alternative.

And instantly I know that it isn't for me. There are all kinds of callings, but there is nothing I would rather do.

When he gets up to leave, I shake his hand warmly and wish him the best of the season. After all we are both in the business of selling whole life.

Where

Ultima Thule

*I*t has been cold lately, but it could get colder. What was it Wednesday? Nine below? In Uummannaq, Greenland, it's often thirty below, and the days are pretty short. Actually it's perpetual night from now until February, when the first daylight will last, oh, about seven minutes. The people there will come out together to see their shadows (really, just like Groundhog Day) and watch them disappear. Farther north, the town of Thule will not see light till three weeks after that.

On ancient maps, the limits were marked: "Beyond this point lie dragons." To the north was the mythical point called Thule, supposed to be a six-day sail from Britain. As explorers pushed into those regions, they dreamed, and poets dreamed, of something farther—of Ultima Thule. Longfellow wrote:

> Ultima Thule! Utmost Isle!
> Here in thy harbors for a while
> We lower our sails; a while we rest
> From the unending, endless quest.

It may not be a myth. The northernmost settlement in the world, that tiny town in Greenland, *is* called Thule.

But Ultima Thule may be Oymyakon, Siberia, which also experiences a long Arctic night. The temperature there falls to ninety-five degrees below zero. That's no myth; that's the cold, hard truth. At that temperature, the mercury in most thermometers turns solid.

Steel shatters; human breath freezes and falls to the ground with a faint tinkling sound, what the Russians call *shopot zvyozd,* "the whispering of the stars."

Now, maybe you could go farther north than that, but I don't think you'd want to.

—⁓—

Abram and Sarai, so the story goes, traveled from Ur of the Chaldees, a journey that could be measured in more than miles. Ur, whose very name now means beginnings, lay at the confluence of the Tigris and Euphrates, near the supposed Eden. Just over some low hills stretched a vast desert. At its height, Ur may have been one of the world's great cities, with some sixty thousand people. Archaeologists have uncovered a magnificent ziggurat.

Its ruins have survived in part because the climate changed rapidly and buried Ur in sand. The empire that built the ziggurat fell to centuries of drought, as the rivers changed course and desert retook the city. A lament called "The Curse of Akkad" records the drought in fantastic details that soil samples have confirmed. Four thousand years ago, Abram may have left Ur with his father and become "a wandering Aramean" because that drought had already begun.

There must have been a compelling reason indeed for him and Sarai to go a thousand miles away. The city of Haran bore the name of his grandfather, and the people worshipped the moon, as did the people of Ur; so Abram and Sarai may have felt at home. But if they had thought that this was the end of their journey, they were in for a jolt, for when Abram was seventy-five, God told him to leave Haran.

With remarkable faith, this man and wife who had spent all their lives in large cities now moved about as nomads in a tent, traveling by stages through the land that would become Israel. Someday, God promised, it would belong to their offspring. In their time, however, the weather changed and the land was hit with famine. They took refuge next in Egypt.

Egypt, a treacherous place, would have seemed the ultimate test—only it was not. A plague, significantly, struck there too, indicating that they had much farther to go. Upon leaving Egypt, Abram and his nephew Lot chose where they would settle, and Lot took what looked to be the more fertile plains by the Jordan. But that landscape changed; the cities of the plain would be laid waste; the lush land that Lot had chosen turned to desert, marked by pillars of salt known to this day as "Lot's wife."

It was against this backdrop of infertility—infertile land, dying cities—that God made the incredible promise to Abram and Sarai that their descendants would outnumber the stars.

> He brought him outside and said, "Look toward heaven and count the stars, if you are able to count them." Then he said to him, "So shall your descendants be." And he believed the LORD; and the LORD reckoned it to him as righteousness. (Genesis 15:5–6)

This was a dress rehearsal for Hebrew history. The wandering, the dangerous sojourn in Egypt, a plague, a miraculous birth, and promises that would be realized by later generations—all those elements were here. Abram and Sarai set the pattern for others who would leave home to follow God, from Jacob to Jacob's grandson Joseph, Moses, Mary and Joseph, the Magi, Jesus, Peter, Paul, as they ventured far from the familiar.

Being taken to such extremes can either disorient or focus you. At the farthest points north, in the long Arctic night, some folks find their spirits and their body clocks depressed; they sleep like bears; others find their senses and their minds sharpened. It's all in how you respond. Some folks go crazy from the seeming isolation, and some folks hear the whispering of the stars.

—∿—

There is another legend about an Ultima Thule—about a cave by that name outside the town of Vadsø in northern Norway. In the Middle Ages this cave was believed to be the entrance of evil spirits to our world. According to the legend, the Vatican even sent a monk to count the number of devils coming through Ultima Thule.

Evil would pursue Abram's family, too. The book of Genesis recounts a harrowing message much worse than a nightmare:

> As the sun was going down, a deep sleep fell upon Abram, and deep and terrifying darkness descended upon him. Then the LORD said to Abram, "Know this for certain, that your offspring shall be aliens in a land that is not theirs, and shall be slaves there, and they shall be oppressed for four hundred years; but I will bring judgment on the nation that they serve, and afterward they shall come out with great possessions. As for yourself, you shall go to your ancestors in peace; you shall be buried in a good old age. And they shall come back here in the fourth generation; for the iniquity of the Amorites is not yet complete."
>
> When the sun had gone down and it was dark, a smoking fire pot and a flaming torch passed between these pieces. On that day the LORD made a covenant with Abram. (Genesis 15:12–18)

Now this was very curious. Darkness descended on Abram, and he fell into a deep sleep—only to wake and find a second sundown.

Talk about disorienting! It would have been like the darkness at the farthest north. Yet the experience was entirely true to Israel's experience. It would be a long night indeed before the wandering ceased, the oppression ended, and this chosen family enjoyed, briefly, *shabat shalom,* sabbath peace.

In the meantime, whenever darkness fell on Abram or his people, the stars of the promise came out.

Well, we all have a long ways to go. We are traveling from the world we know into one we don't—and it's frightening. Given a choice, most of us would prefer even heart trouble, money worries, and irritable children to what we might find after this life. The grave's a fine and private place, but none, I think, do there embrace. The old maps can't tell us what lies beyond that point; all they can provide are legends.

Two thousand years ago, Jesus set out for Ultima Thule. His disciples had traveled with him for several years through small towns and lodged with anyone who would have them. For a time he had even sent them out in pairs, trusting to strangers for their provision. Now, marching into Jerusalem as a ragtag army, they knew they had come to the end of the line, for Jesus had told them he was going to his death. (*His* death? What about them?) In an upper room provided by friends known only to him, he spoke about continuing on alone, as if he were going someplace. They should not be afraid. He made it sound like the most fantastic part of the journey yet.

The bravest among them cried, "Lord, we do not know where you are going. How can we know the way?"

And he said, "I am the way, and the truth, and the life."

Someday we will follow where Abram, Sarai, and Jesus have gone, whether we're ready or not. We have gone a long ways with God, but chances are we haven't yet seen the hardest or the best. The lowest temperature ever recorded on earth was $-129°$ F at the Russian base in Antarctica. Antarctic explorers have told of cold so severe that it shattered their teeth and froze their eyelids shut. The ice rises as high as the Alps, but for all the frozen water, the South Pole is as dry as a desert. In fact, one interior region has not seen rainfall in the last two million years, and every bit of moisture—every bit of ice or snow—has been scoured away. Amazingly at the frontiers, where the light gets tricky and the instruments don't work, explorers say they feel more alive.

We will find out for ourselves. Someday everything we know will all melt or dry up as the dew, for as Longfellow said, we are on an "unending, endless quest." However far we have come, we have farther to go, because this is not our ultimate destination.

Listen to the strange sounds: *shopot zvyozd, shabat shalom.* Listen, listen to the whispering of the stars. . . .

Nowhere to Go but Up

*T*he creek near my boyhood home flooded in the springtime, and of course that was when a ten-year-old boy would dream of swinging out over it on the rope hanging from an oak. Once, full of foolishness and courage, I put my foot into the slipknot, pushed out over the roaring flood, lost my grip on the rope, and toppled over, dangling by the one foot. My parents never knew about it.

While we kids were fishing we might see water moccasins gliding by, and once I saw in a hollow tree a black widow spider, her telltale red hourglass just inches from my eyes.

Just as suddenly as it flooded every spring, the creek dried up each August, and you could walk along its bed for miles finding crawfish and snake eggs.

Far from home, a large cement pipe jutted out of the bank. Obviously it had once drained something, but now the mouth of the pipe was dry. We climbed up to it, sat in it, went down inside it a few yards. It was dark, and most of the boys were too sensible to go any farther. Or were gutless. To me, the challenge seemed irresistible. All we needed were some flashlights, and it would be like—what was it called?—spelunking. Exploring a cave. We would go as far as we could go.

My brother Tom, a year younger, agreed to join me. He and I would explore the tunnel, and come back and take anyone else who wanted to go.

In the broad midday we raced home and I asked my dad: "Can

I borrow your flashlight?" When he asked what I wanted it for, I simply told him that we were playing a game, and with a look that blended trust and caution, he handed it to me.

Soon Tom and I were at the mouth of the pipe, shining the light as far as we could without going anywhere, trying to convince ourselves and the others that it would be okay. It turned out that Tom wasn't all that certain himself. Well, after all, I said, you can't get lost in a pipe. If we get into trouble, we'll go back.

The first few steps were the best, as we enjoyed the terrific echo.

Now, the pipe was about three feet across. That had seemed pretty big at the outset, but after we had gone along for about fifty yards in a stooped position, it became uncomfortable. And it was nothing like a cave. It was just an uninteresting pipe.

Tom thought we ought to go back. But I thought we should see where it went, so on we pressed for another hundred yards.

We could no longer see our friends. The flashlight was having less and less effect—the batteries must have been old—and cobwebs were getting in our faces. Every now and then we heard a scratching or scurrying.

"I want to get out," Tom said.

Honestly, I did, too. Backward or forward, we had a long ways to go. We caught a break when we found a manhole cover above us; but although I pushed and pushed, I couldn't budge it, and said we'd have to go on. I think that was the moment at which my younger brother no longer looked up to me.

We went on for another hundred yards, and another. We were in so far it seemed there was no point in turning back. What if the pipe was still in use? What if it were suddenly to fill while we were in it, and we had no escape? What if we ran into anything living in it?

At last we did see a little bit of light, and though our backs ached from stooping, we crawled the distance to it and found that it was a storm drain along a city street. Our escape lacked any kind of heroism. A man mowing his yard stopped in wonder to see two children crawling out from the sewer.

—◆—

Whoever we are, we've all made mistakes and miscalculations. We have gotten into troubles so dark and deep that there was nowhere to go but up. As children most of us were self-absorbed, selfish, bulletproof, and made it to adulthood only by the grace of God.

Unless you had a remarkably uneventful childhood, you have a story about playing the prodigal son. Or the prodigal daughter—she's in the family, too, the great dysfunctional family of Jesus's parable. And let's get to the root of the dysfunction: it's the father. As we all know by now, it is always his fault. He lets the child go off with a large share of the estate way too soon. And after the child has squandered everything, become debased, debauched, starved, tattooed with self-inflicted injuries, and has come creeping home, this crazy father plants a kiss on him.

But wait a minute—this is no longer our story. This is grace beyond our experience. Such a thing could only take place in the kingdom of God. Can you imagine a child saying, "I wish you were dead. But I can't wait, so give me my inheritance now"? Can you imagine any parent granting that request?

Of course not, and yet that is just what this father does. After the wastrel son comes home, the father gives him an express elevator ride to a corner office on the twentieth floor, his full inheritance, as if somehow he has passed the test.

> So he set off and went to his father. But while he was still far off, his father saw him and was filled with compassion; he ran and put his arms around him and kissed him. Then the son said to him, "Father, I have sinned against heaven and before you: I am no longer worthy to be called your son." But the father said to his slaves, "Quickly, bring out a robe—the best one—and put it on him; put a ring on his finger and sandals on his feet. And get the fatted calf and kill it, and let us eat and celebrate; for this son of mine was dead and is alive again; he was lost and is found!" (Luke 15:20–24)

Even the most forgiving parent in the real world would scold the kid a little, but not this father. No, he treats the repentant sinner like a king—like a messiah. Really, this is a prodigal father, who of course is God.

While the father exemplifies grace, the dutiful older brother in the story misses the point of grace entirely. For all his lofty disdain, he needs grace as much as anybody. He takes no joy in the homecoming. Resentful that the black sheep is getting all the attention, he complains that no one has ever appreciated his efforts. If anything, he seems disappointed that his own brother has come back home.

What else did the elder brother expect for him? Where else did he have to go? After the pigs and the bean pods and near starvation, he had nowhere to go but up. People in recovery describe this as hitting bottom. From here all things are possible: grace can begin to operate; God's extended hand pulls us up a ways and we hold on for dear life.

Dear, dear life. It seems so much sweeter after we've touched bottom—the mature trees against the blue sky, the leftovers in the back of the fridge, even the gray pavement looks better once we climb out of the sewer.

—⁂—

I've been down there more than once. And let me tell you, if you're down there enough, the echoes can get eerie.

Early on in a four-year lapse of reason for which I was awarded a bachelor's degree, I had a clever friend who could break into any room on campus. Brian often sneaked a gang of us into the kitchen in the dormitory basement late at night for cold cuts, burgers, omelets. One day, Brian let it slip that he had discovered a way into the legendary tunnels below campus.

The tunnels! Everyone knew that those tunnels served as a Cold War bunker and held archives, art treasures, and old furniture, maybe even secret passages to the college president's office. We boys grinned and leaned over the lunch table, plotting what was certain to be a major moment in college lore. A history professor eating nearby listened in, and instead of discouraging us, actually asked to come along. And he brought a second professor to our rendezvous a few nights later at the Technological Institute. In the halls of that vast building, we ran into only the cleaning staff and a few foreign graduate students. Brian guided us through the basement to the subbasement and a hellish furnace room, and then, from his overloaded key chain, he took the homemade key and opened a nondescript door to the tunnels.

They were, oh, about a hundred and thirty degrees, thick with mist, crowded with enormous pipes and such a low ceiling that we had to walk stooped over as the blood boiled in our regretful little heads.

There were no Cold War bunkers. There were no art treasures. We found no connection from one building complex to another. We went along for a hundred yards, two hundred, three hundred yards of nothing but hot pipes, not really sure where we were. At last we found a manhole cover and popped it open and helped each other out into the breathable night air of a parking lot. No one saw us clamber out of there—no one, that is, until the campus police happened by in their cruiser. It was a moment that required a quick decision. The smart guys fled like deer, while others of us—the honest, slow and stupid—stood in the headlights and dutifully lined up for the officers.

"Show us your student IDs," sighed one officer.

We rummaged in our pockets.

The officers went down the line, scowling and checking our cards. We were all panting and sweaty.

"And you," said an officer to a middle-aged man, "who are you?"

"I am a professor of history," he said.

As foolish as we all felt, being caught was better than being in the tunnel. Now, you can believe this or not: at the time I had no inkling that someday I would be a pastor. It just so happened that we had emerged in the parking lot of the seminary I would attend a few years later.

So I have been one brother, and now am the other. It will take grace to survive that.

We are prodigals, all of us, with stories to tell. Someday we will not escape; cholesterol, inactivity, and unnecessary stress will take us underground again. But maybe, by our father's grace, we will survive even that. Through many dangers, toils, and snares, we have already come. It is grace that's brought us safe thus far, and grace that leads us home.

Teeth Set on Edge

*T*hey lived in a kind of earthly paradise, but once upon a time, villagers in Fiji made one little mistake: they ate a Methodist missionary. Had him for breakfast. For all I know, he asked to be eaten.

The Englishman Thomas Baker and eight native followers had offended the tribal chief when the chief had borrowed the Rev. Baker's hat and he had tried to take it back, inadvertently touching the chief's hair. All nine of them were devoured.

That was in 1867. For the next one hundred and thirty-six years, the village lived under a curse. Cattle died, and family lines died out; and as other parts of Fiji became Christian and developed economically, the village of Nabutautau remained isolated and impoverished: no road, no school, no electricity, no running water. Villagers believed that the sins of the fathers had been visited on the children.

So they tried to make apologies. "We believe we must have been cursed, and we must apologize for what happened," explained the latter-day chief. "When we have made the apology we will be clean again."

In 1993, the villagers presented the Fiji Methodist Church with the missionary's boots, which had resisted cooking and eating. But it seemed to do little good. Progress still passed the village by; although Fiji's largest power station stood just a short distance away, power lines did not reach to Nabutautau.

The chief, now seventy years old, great-grandson of the chief

113

who had cooked the missionary in a clay oven, decided that the only way left to lift the curse was to meet the Rev. Baker's descendants in person.

Not long ago, a logging company cut a track to the village, and ten descendants of the Rev. Baker journeyed inland from the coast over mountainous terrain, across ridges with thousand-foot drop-offs. The prime minister of Fiji, who knew better, helicoptered in. They were greeted by pig hunters astride horses, lean men in grass skirts carrying long knives. Two modern toilets had been installed just for the occasion. The village's only cow had been slaughtered and lay in the hot sun. One of the grass-skirted warriors noisily kicked a dog away from the prime minister.

The Rev. Baker's descendants hardly knew what to make of it. One said his family had often talked about how his great-great-grandfather had fallen to cannibals, but "it was one of those family amusements really." As the ceremony got under way, a coal miner from Brisbane shrugged in bewilderment and said, "We just want to help."

As it turned out, the ceremonial apology had been orchestrated by an American pastor named Frank Wilson, whose organization, the fundamentalist Assembly of Christian Churches, rivals the Methodist Church. Methodists still make up half the country, although they have been losing ground to folks like Pastor Wilson. The prime minister owed his election to these up-and-comers, and in his opening speech he declared that what happened 136 years ago "echoed down the ages, carrying guilt and remorse."

The expensive program that Pastor Wilson had printed, titled "Healing of This Land," argued that the village was indeed cursed and used scripture to prove it, citing Isaiah 24, verses 5–6: *They have transgressed laws. . . . Therefore a curse devours the earth, and those who live in it are held guilty.* Pastor Wilson announced, "A darkness is lifting from the land."

For the people of Nabutautau, the highlight seemed to be a play performed by the village youth and the chief, a fundamentalist pastor himself, who carried the axe used to murder the Reverend Baker. The play suggested that the missionary had been insensitive and careless and had basically gotten what he deserved.

As the grass-skirted warriors danced and the children sang, perhaps the most primitive thing was the unchanging idea that we get what we deserve.

—⟋⟍—

Once upon a time, the people of Israel believed that they suffered for the wrongs done before them; that guilt was passed down for generations. The story of Adam and Eve (especially as elaborated in the Christian idea of original sin) says that consequences are handed down as severe as death itself.

But when Israel fell and the people were carried into exile, God freed them of a burden. He lifted from their shoulders what no one could carry, and through his prophets he proclaimed a message that is still modern, which we still need to hear.

Listen to the prophet Ezekiel, in the eighteenth chapter:

> The word of the LORD came to me: What do you mean by repeating this proverb concerning the land of Israel, "The parents have eaten sour grapes, and the children's teeth are set on edge"? As I live, says the Lord GOD, this proverb shall no more be used by you in Israel. Know that all lives are mine; the life of the parent as well as the life of the child is mine: it is only the person who sins that shall die.
>
> If a man is righteous and does what is lawful and right . . . he shall surely live, says the Lord GOD. . . .
>
> If this man has a son who sees all the sins that his father has done, considers, and does not do likewise, . . . he shall surely live. . . .
>
> Therefore I will judge you, O house of Israel, all of you according to your ways, says the Lord GOD. . . . Cast away from you all the transgressions that you have committed against me, and get yourselves a new heart and a new spirit!

And here again is the prophet Jeremiah in the thirty-first chapter, using much the same language—about teeth set on edge and a new heart set within us:

> In those days they shall no longer say, "The parents have eaten

sour grapes, and the children's teeth are set on edge." But all shall die for their own sins; the teeth of everyone who eats sour grapes shall be set on edge.

The days are surely coming, says the LORD, when I will make a new covenant with the house of Israel and the house of Judah. It will not be like the covenant that I made with their ancestors when I took them by the hand to bring them out of the land of Egypt—a covenant that they broke, though I was their husband, says the LORD. But this is the covenant that I will make with the house of Israel after those days, says the LORD: I will put my law within them, and I will write it on their hearts; and I will be their God, and they shall be my people. No longer shall they teach one another, or say to each other, "Know the LORD," for they shall all know me, from the least of them to the greatest, says the LORD; for I will forgive their iniquity, and remember their sin no more.

Do people today really worry about passing their sins on to their children? Of course we do, in psychological terms. We worry that our parents have screwed us up, that we will screw up our children. (Philip Larkin had something to say about that.) And still we do what our parents did, even say the same things they said to us. That's how we wind up suffering a crisis of responsibility, either accepting too much of it (becoming neurotic) or too little (character disordered). It's important to discover that terrible things can happen through no fault of our own, just as our kids may grow up exceptionally well in spite of us. We are not the gods of our lives.

Things probably work out better when we own up to our mistakes.

A few days ago my daugher Hannah brought me breakfast in bed very, very early. She whispered loudly to Rexene, her accomplice, that, yes, I was awake. Actually I lay in bed a good ten minutes, looking at the soggy graham crackers and thinking lazily how I would dispose of them without her seeing. When the television went on downstairs, I figured that was my chance. Unfortunately she came back just seconds later with a handful of strawberries.

"Where are the graham crackers?" she asked.

There was the evidence in the toilet bowl.

What sort of a dad was I? I apologized profusely.

"That's all right, Papa," she said. "It looks like I'd better make you some medicine."

God has a message for us about family life—that once we take responsibility, grace may abound. Thank God, we don't get what we deserve. God gives us much, much better.

Maybe you and your family have been struggling with certain issues; therapists and religious people would have you go through certain ceremonies to relieve you of the guilt. But God has already taken care of it, and the evidence is right before you, in the grapes that are sweet, not sour, and in the simple luxury of bread.

—〰—

Holy Communion has always been a mysterious, somewhat misunderstood sacrament. In the earliest days of the faith, Romans and others listening in on Christians were appalled by this most of all: his followers ate his body! Drank his blood! To them, it sounded like cannibalism.

To Christians, of course, it was a love feast—a simple act of unity with one another and their Lord. It resonated with the greatest traditions of their Hebrew faith, and nourished them like the Passover meal as death itself ranged just outside their doors.

Some came to see it as a way of participating in Christ's sacrifice, of taking responsibility for their sins; while others believed that only Christ could atone, and that the meal was a sign of his grace.

We are still finding a balance between those beliefs. One of the chief tasks of our faith is to help people balance responsibility and grace. There is too little of either today. Some Christians would have us all wallow in guilt, while others cannot accept any guilt at all. The historic Christian message that we once carried to the ends of the earth is a message of grace and responsibility, side by side like the loaf and cup.

—〰—

While the villagers of Nabutautau in Fiji carried responsibility too far, some people never take it at all. Consider a man in Germany who seemed the perfect neighbor—he mowed the lawn for the folks next door, fixed their car, even invited them over for supper. So they were shocked when it turned out that he had fried and eaten another man.

"I have intense and positive memories of him," this German gourmand told the press. "I have his face permanently before me. That's the sign of a friendly relationship.

"I admit what I've done," he continued. "I accept that I am guilty and I regret my actions." Well, maybe a little. His lawyer defended him on the grounds that the other man had asked to be eaten.

Apparently the victim had answered this man's ad on the Internet for someone who wanted to be eaten—had signed a will, sold his car and most of his possessions. The defense lawyer blamed it on modern technology, saying, "Without the Internet, this never would have happened."

No, he wasn't responsible. In Germany, cannibalism is not punishable by law, so instead this man was convicted of manslaughter and sentenced to eight-and-a-half years. With good behavior, he could be out in four. Talk about setting your teeth on edge!

Did you ever suppose that maybe the Romans spying on Communion had it right? That the taste was not supposed to be pleasant? That the body and blood of Christ in our mouths were to be shocking and revolting, a perpetual reminder of the taste of our sin? I don't know for sure—after all, the sacrament comes from the Passover meal, which included not just bread and wine but also bitter herbs and sweet fruits to tell the story of deliverance; so maybe the taste was indeed important. But of this I am sure—this is a meal of victory, of forgiveness, and overwhelmingly of joy. Taste responsibility if you wish, but don't miss the grace.

Christ knows, we do not get what we deserve. We don't always deserve our troubles, and we don't always deserve our blessings. After all, Jesus gave himself even though our ways are savage, and his message of grace is perpetually modern.

Scotty's Castle

Scotty was a scamp; Scotty was a scoundrel. If he had nothing else, at least he had plenty of tall tales, like his namesake Walter Scott, and maybe even half believed some of them. When he bought the house a round of drinks and started bragging, he claimed he'd done a little of everything: harness racing, ranching, railroading, trick riding for Buffalo Bill Cody's Wild West Show—even gold mining at Cripple Creek, Colorado. For years he swore that he had found pay dirt in Death Valley, and charmed investors into staking him, although no one ever saw one of his mines.

In 1902, he convinced a rich New Yorker to finance a mine in Death Valley. For the next two years Scotty placated him by writing glowing reports of the big take, but never sent along any gold. At last the investor wanted to see proof. So Scotty reluctantly boarded a train with what he claimed was twelve thousand dollars in gold dust. Before he reached Philadelphia, he was conveniently robbed.

After that cautionary tale made the newspapers coast-to-coast, you would think it would have scared off anyone else, but it brought into Scotty's life a man named Albert Johnson.

Johnson was no fool. He knew more about mining than Scotty could ever hope to know, having earned a degree in mining from Cornell before making a small fortune through insurance in Chicago. And of course his work in insurance had taught him to spot fraud and false claims. It also happened that he and his wife were both quite religious.

119

For reasons no one has ever figured out, Johnson gave Scotty thousands of dollars for a mine in Death Valley, and waited patiently—even brought Scotty to Chicago to hear how things were coming along. Of course Scotty had plenty of excuses. Years passed without any progress, and Johnson traveled out to the desert to see the mine, but saw nothing, for Scotty had hired men to "ambush" them on the trail.

The next time Johnson traveled out to California to check on Scotty's progress, Scotty proposed a two-week trip on horseback out into the desert, figuring that a few days in Death Valley might finish the old man off. Lo and behold—it turned out that the climate was perfect for Johnson and restored him to health. In fact he loved Death Valley so much that he decided to make a home there.

He knew by then that Scotty had no mine, but he had found greater blessings out in the desert air. He'd even grown fond of the scamp. Remarkably, a friendship grew between the men. When Scotty was down on his luck, Johnson and his wife paid him a little to live on, thirty dollars a month. And when they decided to build a home out in the desert, they hired Scotty to oversee construction. Scotty, a master of publicity, told the press, "The Hall of Fame is going up. We're building a Castle that will last at least a thousand years. As long as there's men on earth, likely, these walls will stand here."

For once, he wasn't just boasting. The house was, and is, a wonder. Built at a cost of two million dollars in the 1920s, the Johnsons' Spanish manor in Death Valley boasted towers and turrets, an enormous swimming pool, and a theater organ with a thousand pipes.

The Johnsons were usually absent during construction, and rarely in residence after that, so Scotty passed himself off as the owner, telling people that he had built it over his secret gold mine.

Albert Johnson thought that joke was pretty rich. Apparently it pleased him to go along with it, and whenever he was in Death Valley, he identified himself simply as Scotty's banker. No one knew otherwise for many years. Newspaper and newsreel reporters and swarms of tourists who came out called the place Scotty's Castle.

—ᴡᴡ—

Scamps and scoundrels live well in the parables of Jesus. Somehow they just don't get what they deserve. If your idea of Christianity is that God rewards the good and punishes the bad, you're going to be shocked by the stories of Jesus, because the scoundrels get to live in God's own house.

Now, you and I have a soft spot for guys like Scotty; we just have our limits. We may enjoy them, even identify with them a little, but we don't trust them, and certainly wouldn't invest everything we had in them.

That's the difference between us and God, and the measure of his grace. When someone comes to us asking for money, we want to know the story, if so-and-so is really in need, if so-and-so is deserving. Nothing bothers us quite like being panhandled by the undeserving poor.

God doesn't care. By now he is used to being used; he isn't at all proud about what brings us into a relationship; and that's his grace.

If God is not proud, then why should we pretend? We of all people should be glad that he welcomes scamps and sinners.

After all, you and I are Death Valley Scotty. We are God's partners in the gospel venture, and there's no accounting for it. Maybe we think we're fooling him; maybe he's not fooled; at any rate he keeps us on, when he could have let us go long ago. We can try to kill him, but our efforts only revive him and lead us deeper into a friendship with him.

—ᴡᴡ—

Here's a shocking story of just how reckless God is with his blessings. It's another parable where Jesus's values seem to be upside down:

> "The kingdom of heaven is like a landowner who went out early
> in the morning to hire laborers for his vineyard. After agreeing

with the laborers for the usual daily wage, he sent them into his vineyard. When he went out about nine o'clock, he saw others standing idle in the marketplace; and he said to them, 'You also go into the vineyard, and I will pay you whatever is right.' So they went. When he went out again about noon and about three o'clock, he did the same. And about five o'clock he went out and found others standing around; and he said to them, 'Why are you standing here idle all day?' They said to him, 'Because no one has hired us.' He said to them, 'You also go into the vineyard.' When evening came, the owner of the vineyard said to his manager, 'Call the laborers and give them their pay, beginning with the last and then going to the first.' When those hired about five o'clock came, each of them received the usual daily wage. Now when the first came, they thought they would receive more; but each of them also received the usual daily wage. And when they received it, they grumbled against the landowner, saying, 'These last worked only one hour, and you have made them equal to us who have borne the burden of the day and the scorching heat.' But he replied to one of them, 'Friend, I am doing you no wrong; did you not agree with me for the usual daily wage? Take what belongs to you and go; I choose to give to this last the same as I give to you. Am I not allowed to do what I choose with what belongs to me? Or are you envious because I am generous?' " (Matthew 20:1–15)

If this parable is right, then in the kingdom of God, Henri Nouwen will be honored no more than the lounge lizard who repents at the end of a louche life.

And if we object, God has a word for us: "Go! Take your things and go! Leave my vineyard. Because this is my way, and I will not stand to hear your cry and your envy. It's not about you, it's not about anything you have done. It's about my generosity and about grace."

Yes, it's completely unfair. It doesn't matter what hour we might first have come to the vineyard. It might have been early in the morning, or at noon, or three o'clock, or at the very last hour. Maybe you're still standing around the marketplace, saying, "Well, no one's come for me just yet." But God wants to put all of us on the work crew, and there are blessings for all of us—whoever and whatever we are.

—⁓—

As its name declares, Death Valley is one of the most dangerous and forbidding places in all the world. And yet a trained geologist like Albert Johnson, someone who knew how the earth was made, could get more out of it than Scotty ever dreamed, something far more valuable than gold, something vital to life itself: water. Johnson found such springs below the desert floor that a generator in the bell tower could easily pump enough water to fill a 270-foot swimming pool. An indoor waterfall kept the house cool.

What artistry went into this castle! All the beams were hand carved; the leather curtains were engraved. The various wings were filled with music from the organ, a piano, and a carillon, all run on rolls of punched paper. The sleeping quarters could hardly have been finer. Mrs. Johnson's bed doubled as a writing stand where she wrote sermons for the Sunday services they led in the valley.

Scotty enjoyed the run of the place until 1929, when the stocks crashed and the Johnsons lost a large part of their fortune. In consolidating their businesses and homes, the Johnsons decided to live year-round at their Death Valley ranch. And that forced Scotty in 1930 to build his own little hideaway in a dusty canyon, a little shack with no electricity or running water.

In the meantime, some of the victims of Scotty's swindles tried to sue him for ownership of the Castle. Albert Johnson had to reveal that he in fact was the Castle's owner, and quietly he paid off Scotty's debts.

Towards the end of the Great Depression, the Johnsons were able to take another home (in Hollywood) and allowed Scotty to keep a watch on the Castle once more. He was a hound for publicity—he loved to tie a red scarf round his neck, hop in a convertible, and head off at top speed for Las Vegas, where he'd stir up attention and bring the crowds out to see the marvelous home.

When the Johnsons died in the 1940s, they had no heirs, so they willed the Castle to a charitable organization called the Gospel Foundation, which then took care of Scotty in his remaining years.

For the last two years of his life, he—and he alone—lived in the Castle. When he died in 1954, he was buried on a hill above the house, in a grave topped by a large cross.

There's no evidence that Scotty ever became religious—just as, from Jesus's parable, there's no evidence that the last man hired turned out to be a terrific employee. Jesus's story is not about the boss's shrewd eye for talent; it's not about the worker proving himself in the end; it's about grace. The stories of our lives are ultimately not about our goodness or our cunning, but about God's grace.

God has promised that we will inherit his kingdom. Jesus said, "In my Father's house there are many rooms. And if I go and prepare a place for you, then I will come again and take you to myself, so that where I am, you will be also."

Friends, any one of us might receive the deed. If we haven't received it before, even now the hour is not too late; and then you and I, just as we are, may be able to say, "Yea, though I walk through the *Valley of Death,* I will fear no evil: for thou art with me; thy rod and thy staff, they comfort me. Thou preparest a table before me in the presence of mine enemies: thou anointest my head with oil; my cup runneth over. Surely goodness and mercy shall follow me all the days of my life, and I will dwell in the *house of the Lord* for ever."

Selling the Eiffel Tower

With the World's Fair of 1889, Paris planned to mark the centenary of the French Revolution, and officials hoped to build a tower, the tallest in the world. Despite some outré suggestions (a giant guillotine; a garden sprinkler to water the city in times of drought) in the end, they unanimously chose the design of Gustave Eiffel, who was then best known for constructing the inner frame of the Statue of Liberty.

Three hundred steelworkers labored for two years welding fifteen thousand steel pieces with two million rivets and applying forty tons of paint. High above the city rose the latticework—elegant, timeless. And yet it was not at first popular with Parisians. Hundreds of artists, including Guy de Maupassant, Émile Zola, and Alexandre Dumas, petitioned for it to be torn down. These critics were somewhat mollified that the Tower was to be a temporary structure, on leased property. Gustave Eiffel would get to operate the Tower and its concessions for twenty years, and then it would belong to the City of Paris, to be sold for scrap.

No one foresaw its stupendous success. Even M. Eiffel could not have imagined that millions of visitors would feel that it belonged to them, and would cherish it as a very symbol of Paris.

Still, the French never loved it as did the rest of the world, and after the lease on the land expired in 1909, the government almost did dismantle it, stopped only because its antenna could receive distant telegraphs. Ten years later, that antenna saved it again, this time for radio.

In May 1925, *Le Temps* reported that necessary repairs would cost thousands of francs, and that the government was again thinking of tearing it down. This story was read with interest by Victor Lustig, a con man who sometimes passed as a count. Hungarian by birth, fluent in all the languages of Europe, an observant student of human nature, he knew that all people had a bit of larceny in their hearts, too, which made them susceptible to his fraud.

On forged government letterhead, Lustig wrote to five dealers in scrap metals, inviting them to discuss a possible contract. At the Hotel Crillon, he gave them a bureaucrat's modest little reception of champagne and pâté, thanked them for coming, apologized for the vagueness of the invitations, and explained that what he was about to tell them remained a state secret known only by his immediate superior and the President of France. He said, "Gentlemen, the Eiffel Tower is to be scrapped."

No doubt they had read of the possibility; now it was true. Yes, the Tower was a landmark, but its day had passed. He described the materials and their construction; the total, salvageable, high-grade iron came to seven thousand tons. "I have limousines waiting downstairs," he said. "Suppose we make inspection tours of the Tower." With aplomb and panache, he flashed credentials to the elevator operators, and took his bidders up to show them the horizons of new wealth.

Their excitement was obvious. Not only was this an enormous job—it could make a dealer famous, maybe even raise him above the status of a scrap metal man. Lustig had already sized up one of the five as a social climber and had made him his mark.

By the next Wednesday, he had received five sealed bids. He called his victim, André Poisson, and congratulated him on the winning bid. On Monday, they would conclude the deal.

But André Poisson began to get cold feet. He seemed suspicious when Lustig wanted to sign the papers at the hotel rather than the Bureau offices. A lesser con man might not have convinced him, but Lustig knew what he was doing.

On Monday, he refused to take Poisson's check. He explained that the life of a government official was not especially lucrative, that to guarantee the deal he would require a . . . a *commission* . . . otherwise he might have to consider one of the other bids. . . . Poisson's suspicions vanished and he laughed in relief. Lustig wanted a bribe? Then he was a government official after all!

So Victor Lustig not only sold the Eiffel Tower, he pocketed a large bribe in the bargain.

—₥—

The scriptures tell of another swindler—a father of our faith. He is Jacob.

According to legend, he was a grasping sort of fellow even in the womb, where he and his twin brother, Esau, wrestled; Esau came first, Jacob holding onto his heel. As the firstborn, Esau should have inherited their father's property, but one day, Esau came in from the fields, famished, to find Jacob fixing a pot of stew. Jacob offered a taste in exchange for the birthright, and Esau foolishly agreed.

Esau was a hairy man, while Jacob—Jacob was *smooth*. Their old, blind father, Isaac, meant to give the elder son a final blessing, but Jacob disguised himself in smelly fur and got it for himself. Apparently this divine favor, once given, could not be revoked.

Esau swore such vengeance that Jacob was forced to flee the country, taking refuge with his Uncle Laban. The Hebrews must never have tired of telling the delicious tales of how these two con men conned each other, of how Jacob eventually had to flee Laban as he had Esau.

He had not repented or reformed; he was still a grasping man. At last Esau caught up to him with an army. On the eve of his capture, Jacob spent a sleepless night, and the divine favor took hold of him in a surprising way:

> A man wrestled with him until daybreak. When the man saw that he did not prevail against Jacob, he struck him on the hip socket; and Jacob's hip was put out of joint as he wrestled with him. Then he said, "Let me go, for the day is breaking." But Jacob said, "I will not let you go, unless you bless me." (Genesis 32:24–26)

"I will not let you go, unless you bless me." But God *had* blessed him, looking the other way when Jacob had taken what belonged to Esau. Somewhere near dawn in a sleepless night, as Jacob wrestled with his conscience, God touched his hip. The contest ended with God the victor, which may have been just the blessing Jacob needed most.

Let's face it, just as the Hebrews faced it—God had blessed a con artist. None of Jacob's blessings truly *belonged* to him. They belonged to God. And it was Jacob, of all people, who began the practice of the tithe.

—⟋⟍—

The ancient practice of tithing is still changing lives. Millions upon millions of Christians and Jews still find that they are blessed when they set aside the first, not the last, of their blessings for charity.

We may think that God is distant and needs nothing. Actually God is very near and comes to us every day with material needs. Even the most fortunate of us are never more than a few miles away from the destitute, from battered women, schoolchildren, and the housebound elderly. We can support churches, food pantries, free clinics, hospice care. Beyond our hometowns, there are disaster relief, medical research, medical missions, overseas and domestic charities.

We have three choices. We could give nothing. We could rummage in the sock drawer for what is left over after we have satisfied and gratified ourselves. Or we could set aside the first part of our income—the tithe.

I realize that this runs counter to our instincts. We are susceptible to the idea that we have earned all our comforts, that our homes and cars and toys have come by the work of our hands and the sweat of our brows, rather than by the grace of God.

Yet all things belong to God. God does not demand a portion—he demands all our love, all our time, all our talents, all our heart, mind, and soul. They belong to him. When we recognize this, we can see what it means *not* to tithe. Keeping the tithe for yourself is swindling God. It is like laying claim to the Eiffel Tower—for it doesn't belong to you; nothing does. None of it belongs to you. To tithe is to recognize who really owns everything.

—ᚹᚹ—

All through the night, Jacob struggled with his dread. It had a human shape. Not since the womb, perhaps, had he wrestled so literally and so long. Yet in the morning, when Esau finally caught up to him, Jacob didn't get what he deserved, for Esau embraced his long-lost brother. Overcome by grace, Jacob said—it is one of the finest verses in the Bible—"Truly, to see your face is to see the face of God!"

We get away with larceny all the time. After selling the Eiffel Tower, Victor Lustig fled the country, but his embarrassed victim never went to the police. So Lustig returned to Paris and sold it again.

In the United States, he eluded the law for years, boldly swindling Midwest bankers and an Oklahoma sheriff. He even swindled Al Capone so thoroughly that Capone never figured it out and even rewarded Lustig for his apparent honesty. He had forty-seven arrests, but no convictions—*no convictions!*—until the Secret Service nabbed him for counterfeiting. And while he was in Alcatraz, who personally saw to his protection? Al Capone.

You can get away with it. God's not going to chase you down and prosecute you. God's been turning a blind eye for generations, or so it would seem. Or so it would seem.

But then again, in a sleepless night, you may find yourself wrestling with God, in the close embrace of grace, and God may touch your hip near the socket, or the pocket.

Let's not con ourselves. God knows whose people we are. God knows whose food we eat. God knows whose clothes we wear. God knows whose blessings we have borrowed. God *knows*. Through the prophet, he whispers:

Will anyone rob God? Yet you are robbing me! But you say, "How are we robbing you?" In your tithes and offerings! . . .

> Bring the full tithe into the storehouse, so that there may be food in my house, and thus put me to the test, says the LORD of hosts; see if I will not open the windows of heaven for you and pour down an overflowing blessing. (Malachi 3:8–10)

An overflowing blessing, indeed. It's more than we can hold; it gives itself away. How does God do that? Well, to begin with, God is very clever.

Firsthand

*L*ike a lot of children of divorce, Tania Aebi didn't get along with her father. And, like a lot of eighteen-year-olds, she didn't know what to do with her life. She didn't want to go to college, didn't want to continue as a messenger in New York City. Her father, an artist, figured that what she really needed was to build up her self-esteem.

So he offered her this choice: She could go to college. Or, with the same tuition money, he would buy her a boat, a 26-footer, on the condition that she sail it around the world. She could support herself, even begin a career, by writing about her experiences.

At first Tania thought he was crazy. She had never sailed by herself. Until two years before, she had never even been on a boat. She didn't even know how to drive a car.

Her father assured her it was doable. Sailing, he told her, was based on a few simple principles and common sense. "It's easy, I'm telling you," he said. "You can read my books. Don't worry about the little things. They will take care of themselves. Think big! Think about the world you would see!"

In 1985, with national media watching and most of her friends trying to talk her out of it, Tania Aebi set sail from New York aboard the *Varuna*. As she pulled out of the harbor, she was still reading a book called *Learn to Sail*.

As the first night fell, she steeled her empty stomach for some pasta. The first swallow made her retch because her ship's brand-new water tanks had not been cleaned of fiberglass, and all her water supply was contaminated. Worse still, the barometer was falling, and she could not remember—did that mean good weather or bad? Then the cabin began taking on water—one inch, two inches, six inches! She pumped the bilge like crazy, raced above decks, and saw that she had left the windlass uncovered, and with every wave, the *Varuna* was taking on water! Desperately she stuffed the hole with shopping bags and duct tape.

Then, in the midst of a four-day squall, her engine quit. Now her only navigational equipment was a sextant. An eighteen-year-old girl who had never sailed before would have to sail by the stars.

The weather over the Atlantic in early June that year was awful. For most of the next twelve days she was on her ear. The boat heeled over, spilling her poorly stashed gear all over the damp cabin, but she kept a good log of her position, and became more confident in her guesses.

Her rations ran low. She should have reached Bermuda in five days. At last, two weeks after leaving New York, she saw the light-house of Saint George's Harbour, aimed straight at it as the coast was guarded heavily by reefs, and got her poor vessel in. She had come 750 miles, had lost fifteen pounds, and in her words, "stank like a goat," but she had made it, just as her father said.

She was learning to sail—and now had 26,000 miles to go.

—ฑ—

Some things we just have to learn firsthand. We just don't know the power of God to save until we have experienced it ourselves. We can't imagine the grace of God to deliver us from foolishness or danger until we ourselves have been rescued.

The apostle Paul had been saved from so many hardships, from beatings, stonings, imprisonments, and illnesses, that he certainly knew God's power and grace.

His fellow travelers, however, needed to learn. Sailors delivering him to the emperor insisted on an ocean crossing at the wrong time of year, heading straight into bad weather—not because they valued their own lives cheaply, but because they valued their ship-ment of corn so much.

As if he were the experienced hand at sea, Paul warned that they could lose their ship and their lives. But he was only a prisoner; the sailors had already decided to run past Crete, close to shore. Soon they came into a nor'easter, which blew for two weeks—two weeks of such mortal danger that they threw their precious cargo overboard and treated this prisoner as their captain.

In one of the most entertaining passages of all scripture, Paul takes over command of the ship simply by force of his personality. He assures the men that God will save them, though it might be necessary to sacrifice their ship. In the end, they all come ashore at Malta and learn of God's power and grace.

The book of Acts is a sort of adventure book of early Christian heroes, some of whom, like Paul, were unlikely heroes indeed. You can open Acts to almost any page and find a thrill. My own favorite passage, however, comes with merely a change in the narration.

Until chapter 16, verse 10, Acts has been the story of other peo-ple, of heroes. Here it becomes Luke's firsthand account. He hasn't placed himself in the gospel narrative because he hasn't seen Jesus, but here he is writing about what he himself has seen and heard:

> We immediately tried to cross over to Macedonia, being con-vinced that God had called us to proclaim the good news to them.
> We set sail from Troas and took a straight course to Samoth-race. (Acts 16:10–11)
> We sailed from Philippi after the days of Unleavened Bread. (Acts 20:6)
> We went ahead to the ship and set sail for Assos, intending to take Paul on board there. (Acts 20:13)
> We were being pounded by the storm so violently that on the next day they began to throw the cargo overboard. (Acts 27:18)
> After we had reached safety, we then learned that the island was called Malta. (Acts 28:1)

At no point does Luke say "I." The most that he permits himself to enter the drama is through the first person plural. Just the same, his account is inescapably personal. I love this story because here the gospel is happening to him. He has given up so much to be a Christian, and here God is saving *him*. We can hear his delight, his pride, his purpose and calling.

Of course, to be saved firsthand, to reach the island of Malta, Luke and the other men had to surrender all they knew, give up their boat, and trust God.

—ᴍᴍ—

Think about your own life—about when you set out on a course that you knew to be risky. You braved hard winds and high seas, even when others suggested a better course through business, or love, or a crisis of spirit.

What do you suppose brought you through? What brought you to the isle of Malta?

It might not have been your own smarts. Maybe God revealed his power and grace to you, and gave you a firsthand experience of salvation.

Consider eighteen-, nineteen-year-old Tania Aebi. She learned more about sailing every day aboard the *Varuna*. She made it from Bermuda to Saint Thomas, and through the Panama Canal. She crossed into the Pacific Ocean, and made it as far as Tahiti. All along she faced hard weather, mechanical failures, mistakes in navigation; yet she was proving her father's belief in her.

Then she came to the Indian Ocean, and *Varuna* suffered such damage from high winds that she had to mend her own sailcloth with needle and thread. Passing through the Red Sea and Suez Canal, she was in constant danger from modern-day pirates, believe it or not; and in the Mediterranean, amid the most congested shipping lanes in the world, her tiny craft was struck and almost sunk by a freighter.

Tania barely made it to the isle of Malta, where the islanders nursed her to health and helped to repair her boat.

The final leg of her two-and-a-half-year journey, from Gibraltar to New York, came in October and November, the very worst months to be on the North Atlantic. To conquer her loneliness and

fear, and to reach loved ones thousands of miles away, Tania
agreed with them to read a passage from the Bible every day at
12:00 Greenwich mean time. They began with Psalm 1. Somewhere over the North Atlantic, she came to Psalm 107:

> O give thanks to the LORD, for he is good;
>   for his steadfast love endures forever.
> Let the redeemed of the LORD say so,
>   those he redeemed from trouble
> and gathered in from the lands,
>   from the east and from the west,
>   from the north and from the south.
> . . . .
> Some went down to the sea in ships,
>   doing business on the mighty waters;
> they saw the deeds of the LORD,
>   his wondrous works in the deep.
> For he commanded and raised the stormy wind,
>   which lifted up the waves of the sea.
> They mounted up to heaven,
>   they went down to the depths;
>   their courage melted away in their calamity;
> they reeled and staggered like drunkards,
>   and were at their wits' end.
> Then they cried to the LORD in their trouble,
>   and he brought them out from their distress;
> he made the storm be still,
>   and the waves of the sea were hushed.
>   Psalm 107:1–3, 23–29

On November 6, 1987, Tania Aebi proved her father right—she
made landfall at New York. He fought through the crowd to shout
his greeting. "I am so proud of you!" he cried.

What do you suppose brought her through? What allowed her to
complete this remarkable voyage? Certainly the seamanship she had
learned firsthand, but more than that—she was saved by God's power
and grace. Nothing else can account for her miraculous survival of so
many near disasters. While with each one she had grown less foolish,
and more careful and skilled, really she was saved by grace.

I understand that she is now in her thirties, living in Vermont, married, with two boys. We can marvel at her story, yet none of us can ever know it quite as she does. No one can ever know your story as you do. And that is why we each have to learn for ourselves.

The lessons we must learn may be different, after all. The sailors carrying Paul and Luke had to distinguish between giving up control and giving up hope. "All hope of our being saved was at last abandoned," writes Luke, but then Paul stood up and said, "Keep up your courage, men, for I have faith in God that it will be exactly as I have been told. But we will have to run aground on some island."

Yes, we may have run aground on some island. Yes, we may have sacrificed things that once seemed important. We are here now, with good company, and whether we are nineteen, thirty-nine, or sixty-nine, our real life's story is just beginning.

The Capsized Boat

*C*ome into the vast cathedral and admire the soaring ceiling. Ribs of stone rise past richly detailed stained-glass windows, then join at the top in a long arch. The shape of this place recalls something, which you see as soon as your guide mentions it.

Like many a Gothic church, this cathedral looks like a boat turned upside down. In the early days of the faith, your guide says, Christians would hide from the Romans under boats, and to this day the congregation sits in an area called the *nave,* from the same word that gives us *navy.*

It's an unsettling but a wonderful thought—that the walls of the sanctuary are actually a hull, and that the ship of the faithful is not meant to stand still, but move forward; that we in the pews are supposed to be rowing together; and that we plow not through blue waters but blue heavens.

As you look up and consider all this, your head spins. Either we are meant to be upside down in relation to the outside culture, or the church has capsized.

—⋙—

If you come back to the cathedral on a Sunday morning and see the empty pews, you might well think that it has spilled its passengers. For thirty years, the mainline church has been losing them— and has grown ever more fearful of evangelism. Where once this

137

congregation grew exponentially, now it seems to have capped its size. Some people really don't want it to grow.

The architecture tells some of the story. In newer churches, seating is more in the round, so more people are up close and everybody has an intimate, personal experience. In an old mainline church, some folks are in first class while others are in steerage. Maybe you like it in steerage, maybe you choose to sit in the back of the boat, but newcomers feel a long ways off from the holy happenings up front.

But it's more than just that. Fewer people today think the church speaks to their immediate concerns. They have doubts and want them frankly appreciated, but they don't want to hear some milquetoast nattering about nuanced theology. They have stepkids and stepparents, and friends who are killing themselves in a hundred ways, and they want direction and hope. They also want to be called out of their own concerns into a bigger purpose, but the mainline church talks about concerns so overwhelming that coming to worship is like opening the newspaper again. Inwardly they say, "Tell me something I don't know."

Their biggest disappointment is our anxiety over things like the budget, and for that reason they may gravitate to places seemingly without anxieties, churches that exude confidence. Mainline churches, even the strongest ones, often have an undercurrent of helplessness.

So the old cathedral may not seem so reliable. You'd think from the panic that this was the end of us. Well, I, for one, don't intend to go down with the ship as the band plays "Nearer, My God, to Thee." I want us to call on the one who will get us to our destination, who is greater than the winds and the waves and even our doubts.

Our scriptures tell this chastening, heartening story:

One day he got into a boat with his disciples, and he said to them, "Let us go across to the other side of the lake." So they put out, and while they were sailing he fell asleep. A windstorm swept down on the lake, and the boat was filling with water, and they were in danger. They went to him and woke him up, shouting, "Master, Master, we are perishing!" And he woke up and rebuked the wind and the raging waves; they ceased, and there was a calm. He said to them, "Where is your faith?" They were afraid and amazed, and said to one another, "Who then is this, that he commands even the winds and the water, and they obey him?" (Luke 8:22–25)

How strange that Jesus is asleep! It's the first time we see him at rest, and it couldn't come at a stranger time. With a storm brewing and the boat heaving, he seems somewhere else entirely, in a realm of otherworldly peace.

It's as if he's not even there. The disciples cry, "Master, Master, we are perishing!" They have *Jesus* in the boat, but they are overcome with fear and doubt—just as when we're beset with storms, we can be afraid that God is asleep. That's the mainline church today crying, "Master, we are perishing!"

Notice what he does. He asks, "Where is your faith?"

His calm becomes the wind's; his peace becomes the water's. The real storm has been the disciples' panic, and calm is found within Jesus. At least in a metaphorical sense, this is a powerful lesson about mastering chaos instead of being mastered by it.

But this isn't just a miracle of nature; Luke is telling us about the power of the church. The elements are important. Jesus commands winds and water, the elements of baptism.

Someday (as Jesus's sleep indicates) the disciples will have to face storms without him. But even in those storms they will find elements he has transformed. Life will not be life, death will not be death, and his followers need not fear that they are perishing.

Instead, they will find the enormous power of baptism and the Holy Spirit. With this tale of the lake storm, Luke gives us far more than a miracle story—really it is a parable about the church after Pentecost.

So consider where we are today. The mainline church, which has been given all these assurances, should be in the rescuing business. We're *in* the *boat,* and we're afraid, even though we have *Jesus* in the boat. The irony is that people out there are drowning.

No wonder Jesus asks, "Where is your faith?"

—⟨⟨⟨—

It's time for us to be fearless again.

If at times the church seems an unpromising vessel, with a completely different outlook than anyone else's, well, it's true—we *are* upside down in relation to the culture. But really (and this is the crucial thing to remember) we are the ones who are right side up. We know up from down when it comes to material things that cannot satisfy or identify us, when it comes to wars that cannot be fought without compromising us. The culture leaves people drowning in the wrong answers to the wrong questions, with the wrong leaders appealing to the wrong instincts, inflicting wrong upon wrong.

I would be a lot more worried about us if we lost that distinctive, prophetic vision. As it is, we may be better off without mass appeal. When we're courting public opinion, it's too tempting for us to go by the prevailing winds.

If the church has capsized, that means it has become like the rest of the culture, offering no rescue to those in the waters. And if that's what has happened, then someday a big wave will drag us down.

The most iconoclastic church I know of is called the Scum of the Earth. The name is sort of scriptural (1 Corinthians 4:11–13) and means that the members admit they're no better than anyone else. As part of the "emergent church" movement, Scum deals more in questions than answers, meets (for the time being) in a former shopping center, and collects the offering in KFC buckets. Some of this comes off as a pose, but there is also an authentic restlessness. Scum seems to believe that the biggest danger Christians face is becoming an institutional church.

But then again, this may be the most distinctive church I know: it's a small country chapel with a 130-year history that has come out against the war. That's pretty hard to do in a patriotic area, especially when the hardware store owner and the Laundromat owner go to the yarn shop and ask Linda why she's not displaying a particularly dopey poster that combines a cross and a warplane.

"Sorry," she says. "Not in my window."

"After the Latham boy died, we figured this was the least we could do to support the troops," says the hardware store owner. The other man says, "It's patriotic."

"I do support the troops. They're in my prayers all the time. Why would you think otherwise?"

As customers brush past Linda, the men raise their voices, expecting she'll be too embarrassed to match their volume. They want to know what the big deal is.

"If you must ask, it's my faith. I can't put the cross with those other things. To me that's just . . . sacrilegious."

Now they know. It's that crazy liberal mainline church. "Do you go to *that church?*"

She is fearless. "Yes. Yes, I do. And Jesus goes there, too."

As long as people are willing to stand up like that, I believe we have not yet capsized. We have not capitulated. We have Jesus in the boat—and even if it looks at times like we're not succeeding by worldly standards, that fearless perspective, which he called the kingdom of God, will rescue a lot of sinking souls.

The Voice of One

A little over a century ago the World's Fair came to St. Louis, and it was an enormous success. People sang, "Meet me in St. Louie, Louie, meet me at the Fair." There were such huge crowds that the ice-cream vendors ran out of cups and asked for help from the vendors of Belgian waffles, thereby inventing ice-cream cones.

This Fair dedicated to science and progress had enlisted anthropologists to find "freaks and types from every land" for an exhibit of humans from the "least advanced" to the "dominant white race." That summer they displayed the Indian chief Geronimo as a prisoner of war; he sold arrowheads and autographed pictures of himself. Next to him they displayed pygmies imported from the Belgian Congo.

For a nickel, a pygmy boy named Ota Benga would smile and show a terrifying row of teeth. They had been filed for cosmetic effect, like a pierced ear, but the Fair advertised him as a cannibal and made him a star attraction. On September 4, 1904, the *St. Louis Post-Dispatch* ran an article entitled

OTABENGA, DEVOURER OF HUMAN FLESH

Otabenga himself looks harmless enough. He is gentle and graceful, and the first impulse of the visitor is to pet him and exclaim: "Poor little fellow; he looks so sad and lonely." But look at his teeth! Perhaps he's lonesome because he is deprived of his native food.[13]

142

The newspaper listed some "facts" about pygmies: "They are cruel, finding delight in torturing animals. If they are caught young, they are said to make excellent servants."

After the Fair, the other pygmies were returned to the Congo, but Ota Benga was fascinated with America. He wished to stay here and learn. The anthropologist who had brought him to the States arranged for him to go to New York City, where he was put to work as a water boy in the newly opened Bronx Zoo.

The director of the zoo, William T. Hornaday, proved a canny promoter. In the dog days of August attendance dropped so low that the new zoo almost closed, but when Hornaday learned of this water boy who was sleeping each night in the bushes, he shrewdly seized his opportunity.

Hornaday offered Ota a cage in the monkey house, next to the orangutan. He put up a sign that said CANNIBAL and even placed bones in the cage to heighten the impression of savagery.

Huge crowds flocked to the zoo. Boys would tease Ota with sticks and taunts until he became enraged and bared his teeth. Black ministers in New York City protested, but Hornaday responded, "Why, we are taking excellent care of the little fellow, and he is a great favorite of everyone connected with the zoo. He has one of the best rooms in the primate house."

As the crowds kept coming, the mayor's office referred protestors to the Zoological Society. One of the many visitors to the zoo that summer was a six-year-old girl from Atlanta, Georgia, named Margaret Mitchell, who would later write *Gone with the Wind*.

—◇—

In every generation, there is a voice of one, called by God to a singular life. The gospel of Mark begins with "the voice of one crying out in the wilderness: 'Prepare the way of the Lord, make his paths straight.'"

Such a man was John the Baptist. He was not an easy man to like. He spoke hard truths, calling his generation a "brood of vipers," referring to the Near Eastern legend that scorpions eat their way out of their mothers and are born orphans. John believed that the Jews of his day were spiritual orphans who no longer deserved to be called children of Abraham.

John the Baptist believed that his generation would be gone with the winds of change—that is, with the Holy Spirit. "The one who is more powerful than I is coming after me; I am not worthy to stoop down and untie the thong of his sandals," he said. "I have baptized you with water, but he will baptize you with the Holy Spirit."

Huge crowds came out to hear him preach about righteousness and justice. When he spoke of straightening out "crooked paths," they knew he meant not only private sins, but also the public scandal of Herod Antipas, who had stolen away his brother's wife, Herodias, and married her. Fearful of his growing power, Herod Antipas eventually locked him up in Machaerus, a hilltop fortress.

The cell may have been below ground, covered with an iron grate, musty and dark. For close to a year, this singular man sat in solitude, waiting for word from the outside.

Far from the healing sun of the desert, he thought about the crowds he had baptized. What would become of them now?

At last two men brought him word of Jesus, who carried on the Baptist's message of justice, though in a very different way. John had denied himself worldly pleasures; Jesus did not. John had been careful about his company; Jesus was not. "If he is to wax, then I must wane," the Baptist said. Like so many people of faith, he could see the promised land, but would not get there. Herodias wanted him dead.

Imagine the end of the Baptist's career: where once he had cried out to thousands, now he preached only to his captors. The Romans had treated the Jews cruelly for centuries—had scarcely thought of them as human—and you can imagine how they treated this one, taunting him through the bars of his cell.

And you can imagine his voice coming up through the grate, as he cried out God's dream, God's dream.

—m—

As a young girl, Margaret Mitchell was called Peggy. The great-granddaughter of a Methodist pastor, the child of one of Atlanta's leading families, she grew up in a large white-columned home that became the model for Tara. Peggy was a debutante and, like Scarlett O'Hara, a flirt.

All her life she was confronted with questions of race. In 1906, Atlanta suffered a terrible race riot. While she was a college student at Smith, she quit a history course when she discovered that a black student was also enrolled.

As we read *Gone with the Wind* or watch the movie, we may get so caught up in its great characters and story that we miss its racism. Many fans seem unaware, for example, that Rhett Butler and Ashley Wilkes are members of the Klan. Then again, some of Mitchell's attitudes troubled even her editors, who suggested that she delete descriptions of Mammy's "ape face" and "black paws." Ever the lady, Margaret Mitchell apologized, saying she "meant no disrespect," and wrote instead of "Mammy's kind black face, sad with the uncomprehending sadness of a monkey's face."

She preferred to minimize the extent of slavery and its harms, and never depicted it as an injustice. Her childlike black characters support the Confederacy and choose to serve their former masters. Supposedly farsighted white characters dismiss Reconstruction and the black vote as "darky government."

Peggy Mitchell simply couldn't see Southern history for what it was, and while she gained a mass audience (*Gone with the Wind* is the most popular American novel of all time), she lacked a vision for her own time. Despite her intention of breaking with Southern literary stereotypes, the very title of her novel pined for a vanished past—a past that really never was.

It's hard to see a society clearly when one is immersed in it. Many white people today have a hard time recognizing racism. Even when it's as large as a billboard. Not all that long ago, tens of thousands of cars each day passed a billboard outside one of the Chicago housing projects; obviously meant for well-to-do commuters, it showed a cell phone and asked, *What's for dinner?*

That highway doesn't run straight—in fact it's a little crooked, because it was built in part to segregate Chicago's South Side. The housing projects, too, were designed to keep the poorest blacks away from whites. Those projects are coming down now, but too many black families are still imprisoned in poverty.

Isolated in his jail cell, John the Baptist could only dream of the day that his country would experience the Holy Spirit. For him that dream may have been very specific. Poverty and oppression had so corrupted the people's spirits that they had had to ask him what to do in ordinary situations. They needed radical change, something that went to the root, which may be why the Baptist had so many questions about Jesus.

One thing that Baptists knew then and know now is that baptism requires faith in the winds of change. You didn't get baptized by John the Baptist, and you don't get baptized today, for just the same-old same-old. We have not been baptized to work at the mere margins of race relations. We must go to the root of our problems.

How long will we have to talk about race? A long while, probably. It is the central fact of American life. We do not always want to hear it. Every now and then, God raises up a prophet to help us hear the voices of many.

—m—

After his experience in the Bronx Zoo, Ota Benga was sent to Lynchburg, Virginia, where his American sponsors were sure he could find peace and enjoy the wilderness he missed so much.

Along the way he changed his name to Otto Bingo—a name not too unusual by standards in the South—and had his teeth capped, so his smile was no longer terrifying. He attended classes at the local grade school, taught boys to hunt, and fed himself by hunting deer, rabbits, and squirrels with a bow and arrow.

Once, Otto stepped onto a bus without his fare. The driver said, "Owe me a nickel." Otto offered him an egg instead. The driver said no. Otto reached into a sack and pulled out a rabbit. The bus rocked with laughter. Someone yelled, "Take the damned rabbit, Earl, and let's get going," while another said, "Hold out for a piglet!"

At five in the afternoon on March 20, 1916, Otto—Ota—built a fire outside a carriage house where he had slept when it was warm, and broke the caps off his teeth. He stripped to a loincloth. A crowd gathered to see him dancing and singing around the fire. The boys tried to join him always, but this time he chased them all away. Then he sat down with a pistol and shot himself in the heart.

Margaret Mitchell, however, lived to see her book made into a movie. Atlanta celebrated its premiere with ecstatic events in December 1939. The Junior League hosted a charity ball for six thousand, designed to recapture, in the words of an Atlanta newspaper, "the days when every man was a master and every man had a slave."

Men came in gray morning coats and top hats, women in hoop skirts. The stage had a gigantic backdrop of the front porch of Tara. Every period piece was in place. All that was lacking were slaves.

Because of course no blacks had been invited. So the Junior League had to ask for help from the largest black church in Atlanta. On this night, a choir from the Ebenezer Baptist Church was hired to dress in slave costume and sing slave songs.

Among them was a ten-year-old boy named Martin Luther King Jr.

Do you suppose that this was on his mind when the winds of change hit the South and he wrote his *Letter from the Birmingham Jail*?

In every generation, there is a voice of one, called by God to a singular life that speaks of God's dream for God's people, a dream as yet unrealized. It is "the voice of one crying out in the wilderness: 'Prepare the way of the Lord, make his paths straight.' "

When

Do You Come Here Often?

*T*he old state boat dock at Mackinaw City is no longer in daily use, but on summer Sunday nights great crowds line up for the vespers cruise. More than two hundred people crowd onto an old ferry and ride out onto the Straits, passing under the Mackinac Bridge, singing hymns as the sun dips below the horizon.

I don't go often—and it's hard to say why, seeing as it's a simple and deeply moving service. Surely it's not because I embarrassed myself the first time.

My wife and I had shown up early, well ahead of the crowd, and found ourselves alone in the vast parking lot. No one was handing out tickets. No one was waiting in line. There was nothing to do but stand around, or go for a stroll, or use the two portable latrines which stood back-to-back in the middle of the parking lot.

I went in one while she went around to the other. As soon as she had latched the other door, I stood on tiptoe and crooned into the air vent in my sexiest voice: "So, do you come here often?"

Outside, she pounded on my door. *"That's not me in there!"* she said. "That's someone else!"

I never saw the other person. It might have been a woman or a man. I didn't come out until long after Rexene had said the coast was clear, and during the cruise I kept quiet as the crowd sang hymns, wondering instead if that was the person, or that one, but Rexene preferred to enjoy her secret.

Anyway, ever since then I haven't gone on a lot of vespers

151

cruises—and it's hard to say why. Well, no, wait, I do know why. It's because they're on a Sunday. That's my chief workday, and if I'm not preaching or leading a class or meeting with the youth group, then I'm doing a lot of nothing—watching a ball game disinterestedly on TV, or sleeping. On Sundays I sleep a lot. And work a lot. One or the other.

I hate to admit that those of us who talk about the sabbath do not always live it very richly. Some of the busiest, least reflective people I know are pastors, working from a memory of what used to move us or engage us before faith became a profession. There are conferences all the time for "the pastor's spiritual life," encouraging us to "make time for the Spirit," which usually means making time for another Bible study or prayer group, when what we need most is the impossible luxury of hours for a long walk, firewood to chop, novels to read, everyday sacredness and beauty.

You, too, need what the Spirit offers regularly, free of charge, to anyone willing to wait for a nonscheduled departure. You don't know exactly when the Spirit will take you, you just know that you will be transported. But you have to be in line for it.

—∞—

"The Son of Man is lord of the sabbath," Jesus said. The holy day is for you to live like a lord. All things of heaven and earth are yours: the wheat in the fields may be plucked and eaten by you; that magazine may be read by you; that woman or man loved by you. And if you do not enjoy these ordinary gifts like a god, then you are not getting your sabbath. You are a child of God made in his image, so for goodness' sake don't stagger like a beast beneath your load.

Which brings us to the home of Mary and Martha, famous sisters, famous situation, on a day an honored friend conducted lessons there while chores needed to be done by somebody. Martha did them resentfully while Mary sat at Jesus's feet with the men. It's a situation played out every day in our homes, and here it is in the gospel of Luke:

He entered a certain village, where a woman named Martha welcomed him into her home. She had a sister named Mary, who sat at the Lord's feet and listened to what he was saying. But Martha was distracted by her many tasks; so she came to him and asked, "Lord, do you not care that my sister has left me to do all the work by myself? Tell her then to help me." But the Lord answered her, "Martha, Martha, you are worried and distracted by many things; there is need of only one thing. Mary has chosen the better part, which will not be taken away from her." (Luke 10:38–42)

Now, someone like him didn't come along often. ("You will not always have me with you," he said.) Although the gospels tell of his making several visits to Bethany, and although he plainly loved the family, he moved on to other places. If Mary was to study at his feet and fix him in her memory—this was the day.

There would have been a fire to tend; wood and water to carry; water for the animals, water for the men; meal to grind; loaves to bake; a dinner to prepare for the men who had come with Jesus; and a thousand little courtesies. Some folks like to welcome guests. Maybe Martha could have found her transport in the kitchen, in the everyday sacredness of the flour, figs, firewood. But plainly she didn't. And that's why she complained.

She was busy refusing her sabbath. It had interrupted a dozen chores, it had even embarrassed her, and she just didn't have time for it.

God had made it for her; it was literally as old as creation. When the Hebrews had wandered in the wilderness, God had provided her ancestors with manna, a double portion at the end of every week so they could rest. In establishing her day of rest, God had ruled out several kinds of work, specifically the baking of bread.

But because the sabbath interrupted the things that made her Martha, she was tempted, as we are tempted, to leave it alone. Long before her, the psalmist had gently advised,

> It is in vain that you rise up early and go late to rest,
>   eating the bread of anxious toil;
> for [the Lord] gives sleep to his beloved.
>   (Psalm 127:2)

We are lords who refuse the sabbath. With a high hand we wave away hours of idleness as if they were beneath us; we prefer the bread of anxious toil—more sweaty bread, more sweaty bread.

—⁓—

Why do we deny ourselves a sabbath? Well, let's ask Martha.

She says, now that her exchange with Jesus has echoed in her head a couple thousand years, that she did it for self-worth, for the sake of small pride.

Something within her also said, *You can't sit down with the others yet. Not yet.* Jesus himself was in the next room, and this diabolical voice of duty said she had not yet earned a break. (Which, she now realizes, was exactly the point. She couldn't earn the sabbath. It was offered to her solely by grace.)

She sees now that there was something else, and it has taken all this time for her to admit it.

Surprisingly enough, she may have missed her sabbath because of Jesus himself. He had seemed to treat it casually, so she put it off, too. Until he came along she had observed it just as respectfully as any Jew, as a law, an obligation to God, whereas he treated it as an obligation to human life. And because she had no obligations to herself, only to her honored friend, and because he had esteemed selflessness, she worked selflessly.

Christians have been making her mistake ever since.

He didn't come to the house often. She wanted it to be special. The great irony is that while the others sat at his feet, there she was alone in the kitchen, toiling away at the bread of anxious toil.

—⁓—

There is another kind of bread—which Jesus blessed, broke, and fed to five thousand people. The miracle happened as the disciples worked overtime, after which Jesus sent them off in the boats across the lake to a quiet place for an overdue sabbath. We can only imagine how much they needed it. Maybe Bartholomew took some ribbing for the look on his face when they had collected the left-over bread from the great crowd, and those very baskets may have been lying around. Yes, they had been anxious about how to feed the crowd, but none of them had toiled over that bread.

At last the boat came for the rest of us. The vespers ferry left the Mackinaw City dock sometime past seven, and although it could go quite fast, it lazily thrummed over the growing waves. The temperature dropped and we all huddled close. Wind whipped our windbreakers as the sun dipped below the horizon and the boat passed under the great Mackinac Bridge. Hymns were sung as softly as two hundred passengers could sing them.

A tourist, hearing that we lived nearby, asked, "So do you come out here often?" What she meant was, Do you take advantage of this? Do you make sure not to miss this lovely experience?

And what could I say as my wife held my hand? The sunset spilled across that enormous night sky, all that everyday sacredness and beauty. It is a strange and wonderful thing to be lord of the sabbath.

Now and Then

Now and then we have days like this—distinguished by flowers, music, pageantry, a crowd—that stir our deepest memories. How many things can we recall from the age of three or four, or twenty or forty? Maybe a certain vivid day in spring. We can mark our progress through life by the way we have felt at Easter.

When we were very young, it was like a fairy tale: the pictures of the angels at the tomb and the risen Christ before his disciples— it was all ghostly, and magical, wonderful, miraculous, like the scene within a candy egg.

But then not too much later we began to doubt and asked, Could it really have happened like that? Isn't this really just a legend?

Then sometime later on, when our adult lives began to fracture at the stress points and death became more real, we may have taken another look at the Easter story. Maybe you're one of those who come to worship now and then, and you're wondering if the old stories might really be true, true enough to take hold of your life and change it. And you might wonder, if it were true, what that would mean for you today. Because supposedly it all happened long ago; that was then.

Well, actually, no. Easter is *now. Then* was another time entirely.

—m—

. . . *Then* the people of Palestine lived in dread that the Roman occupation would crush their country. Observant Jews waited for a king who would lead their country back to political independence. They expected that the throne of David would be restored, the Romans would make their exit, and the country would be glorified.

There had been false messiahs before; the people had all been disappointed before. Indeed they were becoming conditioned to disappointment.

Along came Jesus, whose followers resembled a small army. Upon his entrance to Jerusalem, great crowds even acclaimed him as their king, their messiah. But later on that week, it became clear even to them that Jesus was not that kind of messiah. Apparently he was instead a rabble-rouser, a pretender, a suicide who would push the Romans to the limit but wouldn't mobilize force. Conditioned as they were to disappointment, the people of Jerusalem knew how to turn on him. When Pilate offered them the choice of Jesus or Barabbas, they had a convenient way of venting their anger.

Two thousand years ago, this young rabbi was nailed to a cross, hung up between two enemies of the state, though he had committed no crime that we would recognize. *Then* the cross had no religious significance. It was simply the cruelest, most humiliating way to execute someone slowly. As he hung naked before his mother and the few friends who remained, his chest rose and fell, rose and fell, until his lungs gave out; and when he was dead, he was brought down from the cross and put in a tomb, which was sealed. And it seemed that that was the end of that.

. . . *Then* was also just last month, when your friends' youngest child went in for tests to rule out something serious. Just five years old, this delicate boy had started suffering seizures at bedtime, and your friends had come unglued. They would lie in bed with him, waiting for something terrible to happen. Balanced against what they were hearing from neurologists, your hopeful words seemed, even to your ears, pitifully inadequate.

Then was also the birthday that called into question what you were doing with your life.

Then was when you had a falling-out with an old but difficult friend.

Maybe sometime back, you and a spouse went separate ways; and ever after, you have been trying to put your life together again. But it's been hard. The wound has not really healed. You'd like it to be right if it could, but you're not sure that it possibly could.

Whatever it was—that was *then*. This is *now*.

Now Christ has been raised from the dead. Fresh air and sunlight pour into the empty tomb; folded grave clothes say that you really can have forgiveness and hope. Now your life may be made whole again, right again, free again. . . .

It can be true for you, if you let the past be the past.

—m—

Let's talk about now. This is where Jesus meets you—not in the past, but the present. This is his territory.

Today some women went to a tomb they expected to be sealed, and instead found it opened and empty. In horror that the body had been stolen, they appealed to the first man they saw, who might have been the gardener, or a guard—only he was not. Just what he was they did not know, for his immaculate white dress seemed otherworldly, yet he stood solidly before them and asked, "Why do you seek the living among the dead?" The figure continued, "You seek Jesus of Nazareth, who was crucified. He is not here. He has been raised." And before the women could absorb all they had seen and heard, he said, "Go and tell his disciples. . . ." Of course, they did the exact opposite. Out of fear, they fled and said nothing to anyone at first. And of course, they could not keep it to themselves.

This morning you were having breakfast when they burst in with the news. All at once they were talking, unable to tell it straight, interrupting each other. Sidelong glances from the others at the table mirrored your thoughts. This was crazy. Some of the others went to the tomb themselves and did indeed find it empty, but saw no figure in white. No one knew what to make of it.

Just this evening, two others have come back breathlessly from a journey on foot, and told an unbelievable tale—how they have walked with a man for hours *and it turned out to be him.*

You have been brooding here, more angry than hopeful. A half-eaten meal remains on the table. There is a shout.

Now he stands before you, the resurrected Lord, your friend for these past three years, with those broken wrists, that horrible wound in his side, and you want at once to throw yourself on him and to hide. A few days ago when he was killed, you couldn't even stay to watch, you even denied knowing him and tried to melt into the crowd. That was then. Just now, Jesus looks so profoundly glad to see you. He holds out his hand, a solid, veined, muscled, living hand. Immediately you feel its warmth. He has come for you.

—∿—

We are not so different from those people of Palestine. In fact, we have a great deal in common with them. If a lifetime really is three-score years and ten, then only twenty-seven persons stand between us and the people who knew Jesus. We are that close to those who walked with him to Emmaus; that close to the friends who couldn't believe he was alive until he ate a piece of fish, to the stunned fisherman who jumped from a boat to meet him on a lakeshore.

If that's not close enough for you, then there's a lady not far from here who has wrestled with the Christian faith her whole life. "I must have had it all the time without knowing it," she says. "Mother quoted scripture always—it's what we lived by." The Elder Hatch, a short fat man who rode the circuit, baptized her at a torchlight service. As a teenager she answered an altar call, and in the Epworth League she "took the pledge" not to drink alcohol; to this day, she keeps that certificate in her wallet.

Jesus has haunted her, and at times has framed her life so it made a different kind of sense. Not everything makes sense, though. She keeps turning up in Sunday school classes because she has plenty of questions. Her parents died when she was quite young. Her husband died forty years ago. She has no children. But an entire church family looks at her as a saint.

"The thief on the cross missed out on a lot by waiting till the last minute," she says. "Being a follower of the Lord is the best way to make the journey from here to there. And it gets better as you go along."

The path from those Bible stories to ours is really very short. Our faith is historical not to leave it in the past, but to ground it in reality—that is, present reality.

By my watch, it is now eleven in the morning. It is not 1963. It is not 1972. It is not 1985. It is not yesterday. It is today.

We can look back over all the Easters that pointed us towards Jesus, all the days we have put Jesus off. Good Lord, good heavens, we are so used to postponing things. If we want a resurrection in our own lives, the time is now.

The Monarch Butterfly

*E*aster sounds like nothing we know. Good Friday, we know. Two thousand years after Jesus, innocent people still die like moths, as confirmed by any morning's paper.

Maybe you have grown up with your nose in the news and think that the world is essentially random or cruel. If you have made a closer study for yourself, however, you may have found that it is essentially miraculous.

I admit that Easter seems unlikely. The Resurrection sounds like nothing from our experience. Or then again, maybe it does. Come to think of it, maybe it does.

Way down in Mexico, in a remote mountain forest, hundreds of thousands of monarch butterflies are waking up from a long slumber to get ready for a long flight. They are the only butterflies in the world to make a round-trip migration. Three-quarters of a year ago, here in Michigan, perhaps, they fed on milkweed in preparation for the journey south. That was when they were caterpillars, earthbound, unrecognizable for what they would become. They climbed to the undersides of leaves, dangled down, and fashioned for themselves winding shrouds in which they would pass a living death.

When they came out, they had wings; and for no apparent useful reason, they also had grace and beauty. No one had to teach them how to fly; they just knew.

Having come a long ways, now they are getting ready for the trip home. Take a close look for yourself. The air may be thick with miracles all around.

161

—ɯ—

A human monarch depends on predictability. He wants the trains to run on time, he wants order and obedience, a general sameness from day to day—and if anything is very different, he watches it cautiously.

That's why a monarch did away with that troublesome Galilean. Jesus had been so unpredictable that in the end even his disciples didn't know what he would do; he didn't answer to their hopes or expectations.

Once this pitifully passive man in a dirty robe was killed and placed in the tomb, no one imagined that he might come out, alive, transformed, with far more power and authority than any king had ever known.

If Jesus had not been raised from the dead, the monarch (well, a tetrarch and the governor) would have disproved it with ruthless Roman efficiency, hauling the corpse out for all to see. Significantly, he could not do so. Bodies are hard to hide. In a warm climate, they are unmistakable. It's not easy to transport one in secrecy, and the authorities could spot newly opened tombs. Moreover, all the likely suspects for removing this Galilean's body had scruples about touching the dead. The strange situation could not be explained away.

Worse yet, in his second life Jesus did not resemble other living people. He seemed more elusive than ever, so that even his closest friends could not recognize him. Two or more people could attest to seeing him at once, but he declined to show up where the authorities could recapture him. No, the dead were not staying dead and unpredictability ruled the kingdom.

At the same time that the grave stood open, the fields of wheat and barley were ripening. No king had given orders for almond trees to blossom; they did so on their own. As olive and pomegranate trees flowered, millions of migratory birds came and made homes in their branches.

—ɯ—

One of the greatest miracles, and certainly one of the greatest mysteries of biology, is how monarch butterflies migrate. No other butterflies, indeed no other animals, accomplish what they do. Each year they travel thousands of miles to winter breeding grounds. Monarchs in western North America head to the California coast, while those in eastern North America, which are far more numerous, journey to a tiny mountainous region in Mexico.

Somehow they find their way by just a distant family memory. No single monarch makes the round trip. Those who return are three or four generations removed from those that wintered before them. They have never been there before, yet somehow they find the same fifty acres of oyamel pine forest, even the same trees, as their forebears.

And these are not a rare variety—they are the commonest butterflies in the world.

Until 1975, this location was a secret; today, tourists may climb the mountain slopes of a butterfly preserve called El Rosario and discover the otherworldly scene for themselves. The air is thick with wings; boughs bend with butterflies, millions upon millions of them. Sue Halpern recalls the experience in her book *Four Wings and a Prayer:*

> I watched my daughter watching the butterfly resting on her shoelace, watched her reach down and wait until the butterfly crawled up the ladder of one of her fingers, climbed over the hump of knuckles, and rested on the back of her hand. She was completely silent, as if she had lost her voice. Her eyes were wide open, and so was her mouth, and for twenty minutes, maybe longer, the two of us just sat, eleven thousand feet up the side of a mountain, and paid attention. If I were a more religious person I would have called that place, and that moment, holy, or blessed. But my vocabulary did not typically include those words. Still, they were the ones that came to mind.[14]

—⚬⚬—

Truth told, despite our doubts, we do believe deep down in our immortality; we do possess a distant family memory of our home.

One of the most amazing things about Easter is the testimony within us that it is true. It's not an anxious feeling, like a wish; it's a calm assurance that many people felt long before Jesus. Heads must have nodded in understanding when he said, "Unless a grain of wheat falls into the earth and dies, it remains just a single grain; but if it dies, it bears much fruit." The Pharisees, of course, believed in eternal life. But even the Sadducees, who did not, affirmed the scriptures from which Jesus adduced that "God is not God of the dead, but of the living, for to him all of them are alive."

So Jesus did not teach his disciples something new, but appealed to their long-standing belief when he said, "I will go and prepare a place for you. And if I go and prepare a place for you, I will come again and take you to myself, so that where I am, you may be also. And you know the way to the place where I am going."

Most remarkable, perhaps, was his exchange with Martha after her brother, Lazarus, had died. "Your brother will rise again," he told her. "I am the resurrection and the life. Those who believe in me, even though they die, will live, and everyone who lives and believes in me will never die. Do you believe this?" And Martha, whose brother was already noticeably decaying in the tomb, said, "Yes, Lord."

To be sure, not everyone shared that faith. Some objected, "Abraham died, and so did the prophets; yet you say, 'Whoever keeps my word will never taste death.' Are you greater than our father Abraham, who died? The prophets also died. Who do you claim to be?"

The hope of life after bodily death could easily sound absurd. It sounds absurd even to believers—though not entirely. Maybe there's some magnetic compass within us, or an instrument that responds to life's weather changes. Easter stirs in us a distant memory of another home and a metamorphosis.

—◊◊◊—

It's a wonder how things as fragile and slow as butterflies survive, but they do. The summertime generations last only three or four weeks, but those that migrate south may last as long as eight or nine months. Milkweed sustains them for three thousand miles of flight and renders them bitter or poisonous to predators. They are remarkably hardy creatures.

Of course, they need just the right weather to thrive. If it's too hot, too cold, or too windy, they can't fly. Drought or snow can decimate them.

A few years ago heavy snow fell on the Mexican mountains, and biologists feared the worst. An eminent lepidopterist went to Mexico to see for himself the unfolding tragedy. Butterflies had frozen and fallen to the ground, littering the forest floor. Maybe you saw his report in the *New York Times* under the headline "Twilight of the Monarchs." He argued that because Mexican peasants had been logging the oyamel pine forest on the butterfly preserve (earning only a few dollars per tree), the forest canopy had been thinned and the butterflies had lacked protection from the weather. The estimated loss was staggering: some thirty to forty million, or one-third of the North American monarchs.

We get this kind of news regularly. It's heartbreaking, but familiar—another work of God killed by the hand of man.

But a strange and wonderful thing happened. The sun came out, and the snow melted, and the butterflies thawed and woke from the dead. They warmed, and flew—flew as scheduled to Texas, where they laid the eggs for another generation.

—⟶⟶—

Oh, the miracles are thick around us, stirring the air and inviting study. Jesus told his disciples, "A little while, and you will no longer see me; a little while longer, and you will see me." They were puzzled, and he said, "Very truly, I tell you, you will weep and mourn, but the world will rejoice; you will have pain, but your pain will turn into joy. . . . I will see you again, and your hearts will rejoice, and no one will take your joy from you."

Within ourselves we know that that is true. Something in us

recalls our destination. We haven't seen it ourselves; our great-great-grandparents reached it before us. We are meant to get there, too.

In every generation Christ is born, and dies, and lives again. The King of Kings has spread his wings, and millions upon millions of us may follow him home.

Field of Blood

*T*wenty-five years ago in another life, my friend Dennis was a longhaired wild man who loved his father. They often went hunting in the woods near home for squirrels, rabbits, and deer.

In those days Dennis worked as a mechanic, still ran with some of his high school buddies, drank a little, and had his run-ins with the law. His father took most of it in stride, but from time to time he'd say, "You know, I'm not hunting with you again until you cut your hair." And Dennis never did.

As they tracked through the woods one day hunting rabbits, Dennis, stone sober, saw one moving through the brush, took careful aim, and fired. Right where he had aimed, his father cried out.

Dennis found him on the ground, raked with shot, bubbles of blood forming on his nose and mouth. For a few stunned moments Dennis refused to leave him there but had no choice. He ran to the house, not knowing if his father would bleed to death before he got back, telephoned for help, waited twenty minutes for the ambulance to arrive, and painstakingly led the paramedics to the place in the woods.

His father was still alive. Rabbit shot had lodged just millimeters from his heart. When the sheriff came and put cuffs on Dennis, his father roused to say, "Take 'em off. You won't need 'em." And to his son, he said, "Whatever happens, remember this: I love you and forgive you."

That was twenty-five years ago. For most of those years Dennis didn't see much of his father—just couldn't face him. He put his life in order and became a worshipping man, even a pastor, but he couldn't face the father he had almost killed.

—∭—

Everyone knows that Judas betrayed Jesus, but no one knows why, which makes his treachery all the more terrible. Out of our modern impulse to rescue people from blame, we have tried to imagine reasonable motives.

Perhaps he, like the other disciples, realized that their association with Jesus made them marked men, and he decided to save himself by turning to the authorities. Or maybe he was disappointed that the revolution had not come, that Jesus had not been the expected kind of messiah, and so arranged the arrest to force Jesus's hand and reveal his God-given power.

It's hard to imagine that he did it for the thirty pieces of silver forever associated with his name. Perhaps he did it only because it had to be done by somebody. Jesus had said that a friend would betray him, and had told Judas, "What you have to do, do it quickly."

In any event, Judas's treachery seems a very common type. What really makes him such a poignant figure is how he compounded the tragedy:

> When Judas, his betrayer, saw that Jesus was condemned, he repented and brought back the thirty pieces of silver to the chief priests and the elders. He said, "I have sinned by betraying innocent blood." But they said, "What is that to us? See to it yourself." Throwing down the pieces of silver in the temple, he departed; and he went and hanged himself. (Matthew 27:3–5)

We all carry enough despair from day to day that we can imagine some of what Judas felt, just as we can put ourselves in Peter's shoes when he heard the cock crow. And most of us are also guilty of suicide in a degree, because we are unable to accept forgiveness. Time runs through our fingers as we waste opportunities to fix relationships with a friend or a family member who cannot really be called a close relative.

It is one thing to feel such common despair, the kind we all live with. But Judas couldn't bear having the blood of a messiah on his hands. "Anyone hung on a tree is under God's curse," says Deuteronomy 21:23. According to one tradition, he chose an end like that of Jesus, hanging himself on a tree—certain that he was beyond redemption.

—⁂—

In his tale "The Legend of St. Julian Hospitator," Gustave Flaubert brilliantly portrays medieval bloodthirst and the search for redemption. At Julian's birth, his noble parents receive two prophecies: that he will be a saint, and that he will cause much bloodshed. One day in the family chapel, the boy spies a mouse, and more out of curiosity than sadism he taps its head, accidentally killing it. Soon after he throws a stone at a pigeon and feels a spasm of pleasure. As the son of a nobleman, he learns to ride with falcons and hounds and becomes an avid hunter, satisfied with no amount of game. In one nightmarish orgy of violence, young Julian hunts until the fields run with blood, not stopping even for a fawn and its parents. Its mother utters a human cry, and the great black stag warns him, "Accursed, accursed, accursed! One day, cruel heart, you will kill your father and mother!"

Sick with guilt and dread, Julian immediately gives up all his bows and spears and refuses to hunt anymore. He even leaves the family castle to forestall any chance of accidental violence against his parents. In his travels he meets a beautiful girl, marries her, and sets up a home. She urges him to hunt, like any other man.

When at last he gives in to the temptation, it leads to disaster, as all the animals he has ever killed come back to haunt him. Now his arrows fall limply, his spears have no effect; before these creatures he is impotent. Staggering home, he finds a man with a woman in his wife's bed. Enraged, he stabs both figures. Of course they are his parents, who have finally found him.

Julian becomes a wanderer and a beggar. He grows old and wishes he could die, until he sees his aged reflection in a pool, a face that so resembles his father's that he gives up any thought of killing himself.

Countless acts of penance cannot ease his conscience. He ferries travelers across a strong river, accepting no pay besides a crust of bread. At last a leper comes, so weak from the crossing that he must pass the night in Julian's hut. The leper asks for some food and drink. His life ebbing that very night, he begs Julian for warmth—a blanket, a fire, an embrace. Julian withholds nothing—and finds himself in the embrace of Christ, being carried to heaven.

—ɯɯ—

There are signs of redemption even in Judas's story, at a place called Hakeldama, which means Field of Blood. If the name refers to Judas's death, as the book of Acts has it, then it is simply gruesome. But if Matthew is right and it refers to blood money, and the blood is Jesus's, then it stands for redemption that has been purchased for all:

> The chief priests, taking the pieces of silver, said, "It is not lawful to put them into the treasury, since they are blood money." After conferring together, they used them to buy the potter's field as a place to bury foreigners. For this reason that field has been called the Field of Blood to this day. (Matthew 27:6–8)

The place may have been so called originally because of the red clay used in making pottery. And how biblically resonant that would have been, considering that the mythic first man had been fashioned out of *adam,* red earth, and the prophets had compared God to a potter. Matthew has in mind other allusions from the prophets:

> So they paid me thirty pieces of silver. And the Lord said to me, "Throw it to the potter"—the handsome price at which they priced me! So I took the thirty pieces of silver and threw them into the house of the Lord to the potter. Then I broke my second staff called Union, breaking the brotherhood between Judah and Israel. (Zechariah 11:12–14 NIV)

Now, thirty silver shekels couldn't have purchased any land—even to Zechariah the sum was insulting—but what matters to Matthew is the ancient family rift between Judah, the southern kingdom, and Israel, the northern.

This matters because of a rift in another holy family. We know that Jesus's own brothers did not believe in him. The gospels and the book of Acts downplay their contributions to the movement after Jesus's death. And when the gospels list Jesus's own brothers among his disciples, they are named at the end, along with Judas Iscariot.

James Tabor has suggested a dazzling possibility: that a first-century tomb in Hakeldama, opened in the year 2000, may have held the remains of Jesus's own family. Ossuaries, or bone boxes, have been found with inscriptions for the (admittedly common) names Mary and Salome, and the disputed ossuary for "James, son of Joseph, brother of Jesus" appears to have come from the same tomb.

If the Field of Blood was the burial ground for Jesus's family, that would unearth all kinds of drama long buried in the story. Judas may have been part of Jesus's family—a blood relative. The gospels may have downplayed the family for that reason. But they could not be erased altogether, because some of them, such as James, went on to lead the early church. Like the other disciples who had failed Jesus at one time or another, they too found redemption.

Even though his father survived, my friend Dennis grieved. When his dad got out of the hospital, he said, "Get the deer rifle—we've got to sight it in. You're the safest guy in the woods these days."

Still, years went by before Dennis could bring himself to spend much time with him. He threw himself into his faith and became a pastor. He counseled others to repair their family ties, never quite taking his own advice. Then his father was diagnosed with cancer. Dennis made regular trips home, taking days off from the parish where he had worked so hard to put the past behind him. He and his dad talked more and more. A relationship often blossoms when time is short—which may be why family relationships are so bad, because we think we'll have them forever. In any event, as they reminisced about ball games and hunting trips, Dennis learned more about being a son and his father learned more about being a father.

One last call brought Dennis home during Holy Week, the very time that he ordinarily would have escaped into his work on the parish.

Easter hasn't been the same for Dennis since. It is inextricably bound up with the mix of feelings for his father—with guilt and grief, as well as powerful love. At least Dennis is no longer crucifying himself. Rather, he can stand before his congregation and proclaim, "This saying is sure and worthy of full acceptance: that Jesus Christ came into the world to save sinners." *Of whom I am foremost,* he says.

After the services, Dennis goes home and carves the roast at the head of the table for the grown children and grandchildren. In the family today, he is the father.

Berry Picking

*T*his is berry season. Thanks to the rain, we've had a bumper crop of raspberries at the parsonage, just as you may have had at your house. Devon and Ann Pettis keep a patch, as do Jack and Chris Hughes, and folks who raise other varieties have said they're willing to share or trade. For strawberries, check with the Gibsons. Dick and Joyce Billingsley have about seventy bushes of blueberries. South of Fremont, Tom Thiebaut's twenty acres of blueberries will yield 120,000 pounds this season. They are enormous and full of flavor, and they sell for the ridiculous price of 75 cents a pound. The only folks getting blueberries any cheaper are the birds and the deer.

Oh, one place or another you can find blackberries, mulberries, huckleberries, gooseberries, lingonberries, and loganberries. A local grower has even let me taste South African youngberries, which are younger than elderberries. If you like berries, quite literally you can take your pick.

—ɯ—

Most of us in this time and place of abundance know God as the source of sweet blessings. Our faith is perpetual summer.

But Abraham, Isaac, and Jacob knew a God who was stranger, wilder than that. Long before we came to the notion that God is our friend, that we should have a "personal relationship" with him, they trembled at his rare and magisterial visits. Angels sang with dread: *Holy, holy, holy Lord, God of hosts! Heaven and earth are full of your glory!*

Generations later, Moses rediscovered the God of Abraham, Isaac, and Jacob. He had known other gods, of course, the reliable Egyptian gods of the harvest cycle. Born a Hebrew, yet raised in the court of the Pharaoh, he reached a point of crisis when he saw an Egyptian soldier beating a Hebrew slave. Leaping to deliver this lone Hebrew, in a sort of foretaste of his calling, Moses killed the soldier, then ran away to escape his crime. In the wilderness, he found a wife, and worked as a shepherd, much as had an earlier fugitive, Jacob.

One day, Moses drove his flocks near the holy mountain, Mount Horeb, or Sinai, where the Hebrews believed that God resided. The book of Exodus records that here, on the lower slopes, Moses saw a modest, a most modest, display of God's holy fire:

Moses was keeping the flock of his father-in-law Jethro, the priest of Midian; he led his flock beyond the wilderness, and came to Horeb, the mountain of God. There the angel of the LORD appeared to him in a flame of fire out of a bush; he looked, and the bush was blazing, yet it was not consumed. Then Moses said, "I must turn aside and look at this great sight, and see why the bush is not burned up." When the LORD saw that he had turned aside to see, God called to him out of the bush, "Moses, Moses!" And he said, "Here I am." Then he said, "Come no closer! Remove the sandals from your feet, for the place on which you are standing is holy ground." He said further, "I am the God of your father, the God of Abraham, the God of Isaac, and the God of Jacob." (Exodus 3:1–6)

As miracles go, this was not grand. Moses could have said, "Hm-m," and turned away. Lots of us see miracles every day without questioning them. Instead Moses said, "I must turn aside and look at this great sight, and see why the bush is not burned up." And this was the beginning of an extraordinary adventure.

The adventure, we should note, centered on the holy God, and not Moses. God made absolutely clear who was in charge. "Who am I, that I should go to Pharaoh and bring the Israelites out of Egypt?" Moses asked, to which God replied, "I will be with you." And when asked his name, God gave the ultimate lordly answer: "I AM WHO I AM."

It was not about friendship. It was not about Moses. It was about God's purposes for an oppressed people who could not bring about their own freedom without the powerful intervention of God.

To be sure, Moses' encounter with the Holy One did something powerful for Moses, too. It reintroduced him to the God of his ancestors after a long estrangement. From this point on, everywhere he went—Egypt, the wilderness—would burn with God's presence. Later on, some Hebrews would take their freedom for granted and even worship other gods, but Moses would remain keenly aware that any ground his feet touched was holy.

We could be on holy ground right now, even here. We may have been a little too casual about God's power and may have missed a shiver of excitement in the divine presence. If we could only open our eyes, God might startle us, too. As Elizabeth Barrett Browning wrote,

> *Earth's crammed with heaven,*
> *And every common bush afire with God;*
> *But only he who sees takes off his shoes—*
> *The rest sit round it and pluck blackberries.*[15]

—⁓⁓—

Now the blackberry is not easy to pick: Mrs. Browning chose her metaphor carefully. It grows among brambles, thorns, in berries of tiny grains. You can put yourself to a lot of trouble for the pleasure of blackberry jam.

Difficulty should make for gratitude. The best blessings are sacramental—they come at a cost, which makes them sweeter. Freedom, for example, should have been very sweet for the Hebrews. Manna and quail, too.

It is possible for us to gorge ourselves on sacramental things and never think of giving thanks. Amazingly, God lets us have buckets of them anyway. Maybe we don't want the fire, the fear, the awe, the life-changing effects and consequences. If we want to keep our shoes on—it's our prerogative.

At last, however, God may lift us into realms we can't take for granted, where all seems costly and sacramental. And when we meet the holiness of God, it is as if we are touched by fire.

Isaiah saw the Lord high and lifted up on his throne, and the angels who sang *Holy, holy, holy Lord* burned the experience onto Isaiah's lips. At Pentecost, the followers of Jesus received the Holy Spirit in tongues of fire. Deeply personal experiences of fear and awe seem burned into certain people.

Consider what happened to Blaise Pascal, the inventor and mathematician, as he enjoyed the fruits of his brilliance. And such far-ranging brilliance: he had solved geometric problems, invented the barometer, the syringe, and the first calculating machine, and shown perhaps the finest prose style in French literature. Coming into an inheritance while still a young man, he bought a large home, staffed it with many servants, and entertained a dazzling if frivolous salon.

One evening, Pascal was driving a fine carriage when the horses bolted and plunged off a bridge; he would have gone over too, but the traces broke. Badly shaken, Pascal escaped from the carriage as it tottered over the rail of the bridge.

Two weeks later, he spent a long night in prayer. Late on that Monday, November 23, 1654, for two searing hours, Pascal had an experience of God. He recorded it on a scrap of paper, and then copied it on parchment which he had sewn into the lining of his coat and carried until the day of his death. It begins with one word:

FIRE

God of Abraham, Isaac and Jacob; not of the philosophers and
    scientists.
Certainty, certainty. Feeling. Joy. Peace.
God of Jesus Christ.
Deum meum et Deum vestrum.
Thy God shall be my God.

Forgetfulness of the world and of all, except God.
He is to be found only by the ways taught in the Gospel.
Greatness of the human soul.
O righteous Father the world hath not known Thee
but I have known Thee.
Joy, joy, joy, tears of joy.

I separated myself from him.
Dereliquerunt me fontem aquae vivae.
My God, wilt Thou forsake me?
May I never be separated from Him eternally.
This is life eternal that they might know Thee, the only true God,
and Jesus Christ Whom Thou hast sent.
Jesus Christ
Jesus Christ
I separated myself from Him. I fled Him, renounced Him, cru-
cified Him.
May I never be separated from Him.
He is to be kept only in the ways taught in the Gospel.
Renunciation, entire and sweet.[16]

This genius gave up mathematics and society life to study his faith,
no longer able to conceive of a reasonable or comprehensible God.
His life was no longer about himself. He yielded to the mystery,
the majesty of God.

When one has had a holy encounter, with the divine visit burned
into one's retinas, it must change the way one sees. After that,
every tree is a cross, and every common bush aflame. Really, who
would want anything less?

God is generous and abundant whether we recognize him or not.
In this good world, you can go ahead and have your fill without
him. The fields go on for acre after acre. We can't even name all
the varieties of his blessings—blackblessings and blueblessings,
boysenblessings and sometimes even razz-blessings, youngbless-
ings and elderblessings.

You can see these things as your just desserts, or you can see
them as sacramental. Take your pick.

Searching and Knowing

So the police finally killed David Woodrow, despite their efforts not to. Everything turned out badly. The teenage girls who said he had solicited them for sex certainly didn't figure he would hole himself up in his home and refuse to come out to the authorities. The authorities, although they knew he had an arsenal, certainly didn't mean for things to escalate. But maybe their armored personnel carrier didn't send a conciliatory message. His mother, despite having borne his emotional troubles for years now, was sure that he wouldn't hurt anybody; she insisted he wasn't a violent man. But then he shot two state troopers.

David's grandparents, members of my church longer than anybody, hardly knew whether to wish him alive or dead for his own sake. Eerily, both wishes were answered. Two days into the standoff, police lobbed percussion grenades through a window, hoping to disorient him, and in a scene reminiscent of the siege at Waco, the house went up in flames and burned to the ground in minutes. Police searched the smoking ruins, but there wasn't a body; he wasn't there.

If you had a reason to come looking for our town, you'd find Fremont, Michigan, in the middle of orchard country. It prides itself on its religiosity (there are an astounding twenty-nine churches for six thousand people) and its remove from the cares of big-city life. Kids bicycle under elms to the lakefront park past blocks and blocks of folks who know their names. There are concerts every Friday at the band shell. The entire county managed

178

without a stoplight until Fremont finally got one in the early eight-
ies. The biggest annual event is the Baby Food Festival.

In this gentle place, David Woodrow became one of the
youngest Eagle Scouts in the nation. (His Eagle project was to
repair the flags and flagpoles at City Hall.) Many knew him as a
bright and quiet boy. In his adulthood, though, things changed. He
was known locally for theological rants in the hometown paper
(many of them, tellingly, about sexual purity). He lost his job at
the baby food factory because he recruited so insistently for the
Michigan Militia. At the age of forty, he supported himself by a
paper route and rode his bicycle shirtless in freezing weather. He
studied theology and discussed it obsessively with anyone who
would listen, aligning himself with an anti-everything "Christian
identity" fringe group so extreme that the militia asked him to
leave.

He was also known for impromptu acts of generosity—giving
away money, offering to fix roofs for strangers, overtipping wait-
resses. He could often be seen walking along the railroad tracks,
still caught up in a boyish passion for trains. His parents no longer
had much contact with him, so when the crisis began it was hard to
take seriously their claims that they could negotiate a surrender. In
truth no one seemed to know for certain who David Woodrow was.

> *O LORD, you have searched me and known me.*
> *You know when I sit down and when I rise up;*
>   *you discern my thoughts from far away.*
> *You search out my path and my lying down,*
>   *and are acquainted with all my ways.*
> *Even before a word is on my tongue,*
>   *O LORD, you know it completely.*
> *You hem me in, behind and before,*
>   *and lay your hand upon me.*
> *Such knowledge is too wonderful for me;*
>   *it is so high that I cannot attain it.*
>   (Psalm 139:1–6)

I am struck by how difficult it is for us to know one another. Our
closest kin can do things that delight and disappoint us, and much of
our family life is marked by what we learn—parents and children,

husbands and wives, all learning, as if for the first time, what it means to be human.

Pastoral ministry presents a similar mystery. We come close to parishioners, but only so close; we know pretty much what they let us know. From time to time we may have the illusion of transparency, or feel that we understand their problems. But time proves us wrong before it proves us right.

Early in my career I counseled a simple man, a church janitor named Hal. He had marital trouble and didn't know why. For weeks, this gentle simple soul showed not an ounce of self-reflection or understanding. And then he let slip that his wife had accused him of touching their teenage daughter's breast. It was an accident! he cried. He had just brushed her! He would never . . . But before he could get any farther, he fled my office. Some days later his wife called me at home. Hal was in the tool-shed, threatening to kill himself.

This situation in Fremont was far stranger. I had been in town just one week when the standoff began. David had been raised in the church; his parents and grandparents still attended. So did the family of a fifteen-year-old girl he had approached. So did several state troopers. It seemed a very typically Christian circumstance that we all should belong to the same church family.

In broad daylight I drove through my new town, wondering what else lay beneath the surface.

Night was very eerie, too, knowing that he might come to the parsonage. Police had combed the wreckage of his home and found no trace of his body. He had apparently eluded them during a shift change. Not far from the house they found a backpack containing a change of clothes, raisins, foil blankets, and a gas mask. An all-points bulletin turned up mostly false leads. From the militia he had acquired survival skills and night-vision equipment, and apparently he was getting more help from sympathizers, because several days after his disappearance, police found near his home a poncho and a jug of ice water that was still cold. So he was out there somewhere.

> *Where can I go from your spirit?*
> *Or where can I flee from your presence?*

If I ascend to heaven, you are there;
* if I make my bed in Sheol, you are there.*
If I take the wings of the morning
* and settle at the farthest limits of the sea,*
even there your hand shall lead me,
* and your right hand shall hold me fast.*
If I say, "Surely the darkness shall cover me,
* and the light around me become night,"*
even the darkness is not dark to you;
* the night is as bright as the day,*
* for darkness is as light to you.*

According to tradition, Psalm 139 reflects a young David on the run from a jealous King Saul. The psalmist is at once naked and veiled. He addresses God, not us, the readers, the eavesdroppers; and we cannot see what God sees. We cannot even overhear hints. Ordinarily, of course, people try to describe and justify themselves, to preempt the judgment of others, but the psalmist does not presume to say what God sees.

Instead David surrenders, turns himself in, gives up the chase, and meets his pursuer face-to-face. It is not Saul who concerns him, but the ever-present God, his maker and judge.

Later in his life, David will forget or deny that the eyes of an all-seeing God are upon him. He will coldly take another man's wife, coldly advise Solomon to settle scores. Apparently this keen awareness of God is hard to sustain.

We moderns take even less thought of a God who searches us and knows us. The profound theologian Max Picard wrote that "the Flight from God," humanity's headlong escape from awareness of the divine, is so pervasive that we hardly perceive it anymore:

The Flight is so much a part of himself that it seems to be the rule and not the exception. When the Flight exists by itself and independently of man, one no longer asks why one flees. One forgets that one flees from God.[17]

We take for granted that all our inner conflict matters to no one. No one sees or cares if there is any wrong in us. So we are cut free from any moorings; the courtyards of the Temple are dark, dark as a godless universe. And once religious persons become a law unto themselves, the Flight from God is itself the real terror.

> For it was you who formed my inward parts;
> you knit me together in my mother's womb.
> I praise you, for I am fearfully and wonderfully made.

David Woodrow was born two months prematurely, and throughout his life he was gaunt and determined to prove himself. He worked here and there at odd jobs, much as his grandfather before him. Even though he didn't have much formal education, he labored over theological books at the public library, and nothing gave him more pleasure than to debate theology with people who had had seminary training.

Between childhood and adulthood, something within him changed. He traded in the Boy Scouts for paramilitary groups, and church for a private faith. Although he kept to himself, he wrote letter after letter to the local newspaper. In his home he stockpiled two hundred pounds of silver coins (believing other currency was worthless) and food for the millennium or a nuclear war. And, as the public would learn, he stored thousands of rounds of ammunition to meet his private terrors.

What changed the boy into this man? Maybe a clue could be found in his insistence on sexual purity. In a letter to the editor titled "Indecency," he warned that the state legislature might soon repeal statutes against homosexuality, and he recalled Jezebel and Sodom before moving on to praise "a judge who ordered a defense lawyer to get rid of a white V-neck top showing cleavage and her bra straps." Even when his subject was lying, he used a curious choice of words: "If we want to cure this social disease, we must remember that children are impressionable." Something compelled these odd essays. How ironic, then, that he was accused of soliciting a minor, and that he felt driven to defend his innocence to the point of suicide.

Maybe it is love that keeps us searching for the truth about each other, and maybe it is our awkwardness at love that keeps us from finding it.

For five nights after David's home burned, his family waited, and it was possible to imagine that he might be on the run for years. Then suddenly it was all over. At five o'clock on Sunday morning, one week after his standoff had begun, police discovered David sleeping in an abandoned car four miles from his home. They shone a light on him and told him to stay in the car. Instead he got out and raised an assault rifle, and they shot him. He had been carrying a map of the county, a map of the small neighboring town where his teenage accuser lived, and tools for breaking into a home.

> *In your book were written*
>   *all the days that were formed for me,*
>   *when none of them as yet existed.*
> *How weighty to me are your thoughts, O God!*
>   *How vast is the sum of them!*
> *I try to count them—they are more than the sand;*
>   *I come to the end—I am still with you.*

I was relieved that he was dead. Rexene and I slept a lot better that night. How horrible, though, how cruel, how unfeeling and unpastoral, to be glad that one of my neighbors was dead!

I didn't want to think about it much, but the thought kept nagging me that what happened to him could happen to any one of us too. Mental breakdowns can happen to the strongest people. And we all have wanted people dead. What pastor hasn't mentally killed off a few parishioners? Maybe there wasn't a great deal of difference between Larry Wood and David Woodrow.

Considering how easily violence can break into our world, there's no wonder that it appears even in scripture. Paul Tillich observed of Psalm 139: "Religious fanaticism appears, that fanaticism which has inflamed the arrogance of the churches, the cruelty of the moralists, and the inflexibility of the orthodox. The sin of religion appears in one of the greatest psalms." The verses really are terrifying:

> *O that you would kill the wicked, O God,*
>   *and that the bloodthirsty would depart from me —*
> *those who speak of you maliciously,*

> *and lift themselves up against you for evil!*
> *Do not I hate those who hate you, O LORD?*
> *And do I not loathe those who rise up against you?*
> *I hate them with perfect hatred;*
> *I count them my enemies.*

As news of David's death reached the coffee shops, differences of opinion came to the surface as if a depth charge had just blasted them up from the bottom. Some said he had it coming to him; others said the police had behaved like storm troopers and he'd been right to fight them. The teenage girls, meanwhile, blamed themselves for the deaths of two men. Over at City Hall, flags flew at half-staff for the officer David had killed. They were the flags that David had restored for his Eagle project years ago.

I lined up some extra ushers for the memorial service, just in case things threatened to get out of hand. The crowd was peaceable, large, and diverse. Longtime church members dressed conventionally, while bearded militia members seemed to have swarmed straight out of the woods, their eyes fierce and full of hurt. Many of them wore black armbands; one arrived with a hunting knife strapped to his waist. I shook hands with a lanky fellow in a leisure suit who leaned in close and declared, "That man died a hero."

Apparently, just below the surface, this community had many David Woodrows.

Beneath every memorial service is the age-old question: How can one sum up a life? Who can take the measure of any man or woman? By the end of the hour, we still had not found him. He had flown the body. If his parents wanted to define him, he had escaped. If his comrades wanted to claim him, too, he had escaped. He had gone where none would follow, but all of us must—to stand before an all-knowing God.

> *Search me, O God, and know my heart;*
> *test me and know my thoughts.*
> *See if there is any wicked way in me,*
> *and lead me in the way everlasting.*

Bride of Christ

*T*he bride wore a white dress with pearls, a veil, and a big red nose. The groom had a rainbow wig, and instead of patent leather shoes, floppy brogues as big as boats which were coming apart at the toes. All around them a raucous band of clowns held aloft tubas and big bass drums.

"Do you, Gilbert, take Glenna to be your wife?"

"I sure do."

"Do you, Glenna, take this clown to be your husband?"

"I do," she smiled, and someone honked a horn.

About seventy clowns had gathered around a motel swimming pool as passersby stared in wonder. One little girl, wrapped in a towel and dripping on the green carpet, wanted to know if someone was putting her on. The preacher said a few words that she couldn't quite catch, and then she had her signal that it was all in earnest.

A big cheer went up in the motel courtyard, and drums thumped, and the great machinery of music ramped into choruses of *When You're Smiling* and *When the Saints Go Marching In*. To which the bride and groom danced, not waiting for any formal party. A few clowns even jumped into the pool to punctuate the song.

I've done a lot of questionable weddings for poorly matched couples with doubtful taste. Yet I look back on that wedding fondly. It may have been utterly pagan, but it was joyous, and Jesus was there.

185

To be honest, most weddings are pagan. Very rarely does a ceremony today put God front and center, and when it does, the guests mutter how impersonal it was. Weddings are, for the most part, unserious but highly expensive affairs far removed from the values of a church. Will Willimon, perhaps the dean of American preachers, speaks for many of us when he says, "Happy events like weddings as among the most unhappy things we do."

Maybe that requires some explanation. But you would understand if you had come with me to a lakefront home awash in thousands of dollars' worth of flowers, with a magnificent trellis that the hired man had just finished. BMWs and Land Rovers filled the driveway and cases of Moët champagne were stacked by silver buckets of ice. More resplendent than the wedding party, and more dignified, caterers in starched white smocks arranged tables of meats, cheeses, fresh fruits, and ice sculptures. All was not well, however. The bride was over an hour late and the groom was plowed. He stewed outside the garage, fished in a cooler for another beer, and mused about her. "A princess in her own mind," he said, among plenty else that was more colorful.

But she showed up before the guests gave up, a little unsteady on her stiletto heels, balancing herself with a bouquet, assuring everyone that the shrimp would wait. All the cautions raised by months of premarital counseling seemed to have melted in the hot sun. Everything had been paid for, so what else was there to do except get them married?

As the bride's ten-year-old daughter processed glumly down the grassy aisle between the rented chairs, wearing a dress too small for her, a boom box played Axl Rose's "Sweet Child O' Mine." Then the bride herself appeared on the arm of her maid of honor— maybe not the traditional way to do it, but they made it down the aisle.

Pointlessly earnest, I did indeed speak of marriage as a holy and honorable estate, not to be entered into lightly. Of course I reminded them that there would be hard days when love would be tested, when the vows they spoke could be kept only by God's grace. "Please repeat after me," I told the groom. " 'I give you this ring . . .' "

"I give you this ring," he said uncertainly.

" 'As a sign of my vow . . .' "

"As a sign of my vow."

" 'And with all that I have . . .' "

"And with all that I have . . . except my boat. She doesn't get my boat!"

For just a moment, I think, the shrimp stopped thawing. The bride's daughter froze. And in the stunned silence, the bride laughed as if her man had said something so characteristically asinine that now everyone knew just what she was marrying, to hell with us all.

—ɱ—

But I figure weddings have always been a little pagan. Even at the wedding Jesus attended in Cana, the party mattered most of all. A crisis came when the wine ran out, and Jesus's mother, Mary—you know, the sainted figure in blue—pressed him to do something about it. "Woman, my time has not yet come," he said. Really, did she think his first miracle should be something as worldly as helping the guests to get drunk? But he relented. And this typified much of his earthly ministry. He was willing to be used.

> On the third day there was a wedding in Cana of Galilee, and the mother of Jesus was there. Jesus and his disciples had also been invited to the wedding. When the wine gave out, the mother of Jesus said to him, "They have no wine." And Jesus said to her, "Woman, what concern is that to you and to me? My hour has not yet come." His mother said to the servants, "Do whatever he tells you." Now standing there were six stone water jars for the Jewish rites of purification, each holding twenty or thirty gallons. Jesus said to them, "Fill the jars with water." And they filled them up to the brim. He said to them, "Now draw some out, and take it to the chief steward." So they took it. When the steward tasted the water that had become wine, and did not know where it came from (though the servants who had drawn the water knew), the steward called the bridegroom and said to him, "Everyone serves the good wine first, and then the inferior

wine after the guests have become drunk. But you have kept the good wine until now." Jesus did this, the first of his signs, in Cana of Galilee, and revealed his glory; and his disciples believed in him. (John 2:1–11)

From here the story goes into the riotous wee hours, as intrepid partyers dance under the stars and Yakob's unmarried eldest daughter pairs off with a young widower. Guests marvel that their host isn't putting out the cheap stuff now that they should be too drunk to notice. The host himself drinks in their joy. It is all very carnal, incarnational, and scandalously sacramental.

Yes, sacramental. This is the gospel of John, so of course we're looking not just at a miracle but a sign, something with theological dimension. Jesus could have chosen any vessels, but made use of *those* jars. Holding perhaps a hundred and eighty gallons, when only a drop of water on the wrist was needed for purification, they would have sufficed for most of Israel. Significantly, they were empty. Sacramentally, Jesus filled them with wine. John's theological point is obvious: *His blood will make us pure.*

And yet—this wasn't blood, this was wine at a wedding, and once Jesus made it, there was no more water. No one rose outraged and demanded what had happened to it. The servants didn't object, either. They all were just having a high old time, enjoying that endless supply of wine.

It's one of Jesus's most curious miracles, how he exchanged religious ritual for simple joy.

For the first time, but not the last, Jesus had let himself be used. It would happen again with ten lepers, and again with a crowd of five thousand who stayed for supper. People who thought they were getting something from him would come away transformed; their encounters would be intoxicating and purifying.

That's part of pastoral ministry—the willingness to be used. Like Jesus, we pastors have plenty of opportunities to meet people where they are and transform them. When parents want a child baptized, we could ask why. ("Why?" they would puzzle, "why?") When two young people come asking for a ceremony, we could instead make them think about why they want to have sex with no one else for the rest of their lives, and what God has to do with that.

There's a lot of potential in these routine pastoral encounters. But some days, about the most religious question I ask is, "Would you prefer the Trumpet Tune or the Mendelssohn?"

Jesus didn't miss these opportunities, because he knew who he was. Despite the dizzying variety of things people said about him, he may have been more sure of himself than we are of ourselves. He was a Jew; a very devout Jew. His message was neither liberal nor conservative, but radical. And he knew that his God was certainly not to be confused with Baal or Mammon, this intoxicating, purifying God—a God of joy.

—ɯ—

My friend David has done his share of weddings, always looking forward to one in particular. He's a big bear of a guy, with a beard and a swarthy face, a useful disguise for someone so tender. No one has ever brought out more of its expressiveness than his daughter Miriam. As a little girl she told him that she wanted a big wedding and he should start saving. Later on she became such an exasperating free spirit that David was tempted to keep her bottled up at home.

"Your dates need to know one thing," he said. "I have a shotgun and a shovel."

"Yeah, they read that on the Internet, too," she said. "Look, Dad, make it easy on yourself. Don't wait up for me."

By the time she was nineteen, Miriam had gone out with plenty of guys and given him ever more cause for anxiety, learning some hard lessons and not learning others. She wound up in rehab, where at last she found a tentative faith of her own.

Two days before Father's Day, she made an unfortunate left-hand turn into oncoming traffic.

In a terrible irony, she lay at the very hospital where David had been a chaplain. Her injuries were so severe that after a while all they could do was turn off her life support and wait. David sat at her bedside, stroking her hand.

A few days later, a thousand mourners gathered for a funeral that was surprisingly joyous, more so than most weddings. For the better part of an hour, a band played praise songs, and we were encouraged to sing, even dance. Some mourners didn't know what to make of it. David managed to give the eulogy—clothed and in his right mind, as the phrase goes, and at a stage of grief that others of us could only imagine. "Please don't misunderstand," he said. "Our family is just stricken with grief. But we also want you to know how it's possible for us to feel joy, too. I really have to tell you a story."

David told of his anguish at the hospital as he had stroked her hand. When Miriam had been a little girl, she had held onto him, and he had protected her. After all, what else does a father do? Their whole life together had pointed towards the answer, but David had not really let her go, for Miriam hadn't met the right man. And now he would never give her to a husband.

Within him, or all around him, a voice spoke unmistakably. It said, *You are so wrong. I have already taken her by the hand, and she will be my bride.*

He knew that this was true.

So did his wife, when he told her about it. A wise woman, she knew what needed to be done for funeral arrangements.

"And that is why," said David, "Miriam is wearing her mother's wedding dress."

Ever since hearing that story, I have thought about it before performing a wedding. The couples scarcely have any idea what they're promising—to have and to hold for better or worse, for richer or poorer, through sickness and health, until they are parted by death—and really, who could understand those vows until living them all the way through? The best that the ceremony can do is hint at the depth of the water in those tall jars.

So here comes the bride, all dressed in white. She's on the verge of a lifetime with a man who is still a boy, and she's worried about whether her caterer has fully stocked the bar. Someone needs to take the water of the moment and turn it into wine. "Woman, what does this have to do with us?" Everything.

The Second Coming

*T*he apostles began the Christian era in a strange way. First they said good-bye. Jesus's ascension was an uncanny farewell, like seeing someone die, except this was the opposite—they knew that he was alive and would never die; indeed, they would not either, so they would fear nothing. This did not feel like loss, but gain.

Just like that, he was gone. Like a wraith, like a dream, he left behind no children, no estate, no writings, no trace of himself except this feeling that his presence was real, that his absence was temporary. The ascension marked the moment when the Christian story passed from Jesus's time into our own.

Perhaps out of a sense of inadequacy, we have been waiting for him to come back and reclaim his story. Ever since he supposedly rose from the ground of Bethany and the disciples understood that he would return in the same spectacular way, we have been waiting for the Second Coming.

In 1798, 1829, and again in 1844, forerunners of the Jehovah's Witnesses identified an antichrist in their times and proclaimed an imminent end to the world. A generation later, a preacher named Charles Taze Russell taught that Christ had come invisibly in 1874; his followers, the Russellites, believed that a period of social revolution and chaos would begin forty years later, culminating in Christ's kingdom on earth. True enough, 1914 did coincide with World War I, and indeed, the next several years did see revolution and chaos, but the world did not end. The Russellites may actually have been disappointed.

By now, we might reasonably suspect that the cosmic drama may not end with a full orchestra, the house lights coming on, the main actor and author stepping forward out of costume, infinitely more impressive than before, bringing all the threads of the story together.

It would be majestic and wonderful. And yet God may not work like that.

Whoever said the coming of the Son of Man on clouds of glory would be the *Second* Coming? What if it is the millionth? Christ may have come without notice many times already. The clouds of glory may be at number five hundred million and one.

In the meantime, we may wait for Christ to come in the way that he promised to his disciples.

According to the gospels, when Jesus was incarnated in Mary, the *Holy Spirit* came upon her. And when the grown Jesus prepared to leave his disciples and return to God, he promised them the *Holy Spirit*. The Holy Spirit came upon them at Pentecost, just as it had come over Mary, but this time Christ was no longer incarnate in just one person. Indeed, today we all belong to that body.

—m—

On a hot day in August, across from the bus terminal in Baltimore, a hotel desk clerk drummed his fingers as he read *Kiss Me, Deadly*. In just the first few pages, Mike Hammer had picked up a dame, been run off the road, and been knocked out. The bad guys had stuffed Hammer and the dame back in the car and were sending them over a cliff when the clerk felt a faint breeze from an open door.

An aging man had stepped in. Unhurriedly he removed his jacket, laid it over a single shabby suitcase, and took off a fedora wet with sweat. "Got a room, son?" he asked.

The desk clerk sized him up. The man's plain gray suit had winkles within wrinkles; he might have been wearing it for weeks. His shirt collar was stained from wear, and the cuffs were coming off. "Yeah, I think we do . . . fifteen dollars, though. Pay in advance."

"That's fine," said the man as he reached into his pocket and pulled out a weathered wallet. "So tell me," the man said, "where do you preach?"

"What?" the clerk asked. For just a second, the noise of a fan spinning overhead became more noticeable.

"You look to be about twenty-five, twenty-six. You've been doing something with your life, I'm sure. Tell me your story."

It might have sounded impudent, except the man was so courteous and his shoes were so worn. With a sigh, the clerk told a rambling story (no one had ever asked before) about how his grandmother had encouraged him to pursue his talent for drawing but he didn't want to waste money on college . . .

The old man followed intently all through the unpracticed telling of this dull story. Then he said, "I'm glad to know you. I'll be staying here a few days, and another time I'll tell you my story." He extended a warm handshake, then picked up the suitcase. "One more thing," the old man said with a curious roll of the eyes. "I'm wondering where a guy would go for a drink."

It was two in the afternoon. Well, if the old guy needed it that badly, sure, he could find a place just up the block.

First, though, the rumpled man checked into his room and scrubbed some stains out of that suit. Years ago some friends had implored him to buy a new one. He had declined. So they had bought one for him, and reluctantly he had worn it for a few weeks before they noticed that he was back in the old suit. "I gave it to someone who needed it," he explained.

Nowadays he traveled the country with no particular program, no set itinerary. Later in the day, maybe, he'd look up a few friends, although anyone who knew him could expect to find him in the bar.

Around the corner on a sour-smelling street and down a flight of steps, he found the place—not too disagreeable, considering. The long walnut bar itself shone, with a rack of clean glasses overhead and a pyramid of bottles sparkling in front of a mirror. Off at a corner table were two businessmen on an all-day lunch, and a younger fellow in blue jeans was hanging at the end of the bar, near the kitchen. The balding man chose a seat in the middle of the counter and asked for a cup of coffee.

194 News to Me

A smartly turned-out young woman came in, smoothed her
skirt, and eyed the room for a place to sit. This old guy talking to
the bartender looked safe. She took a stool two over from him and
said to the bartender, "Rob Roy, please."

"Rob Roy," the man said softly. "And I would have taken you
for Welsh. How do you do, miss?"

"It has been a perfectly awful day, thank you very much," she
answered. "Really, I came here to change the subject." Thinking
she might have been too unfriendly, she amended, "Maybe you've
had a better day yourself."

"I'm sure I have," he said politely, running a finger over the rim
of his mug.

The woman studied him apprehensively, brushed her hair back,
and said, "If you must know, my car is in the shop, so I have to take
a bus back to Virginia."

He raised his eyebrows. "No one to take you?"

"Afraid not."

"Just a short trip?"

"I don't know," she said.

He volunteered that he was a traveler himself, otherwise he
would have offered her a ride. He was surprised that a pretty
woman should be on her own. She inwardly forgave him this
unfashionable gallantry and explained that her boyfriend of the last
few months had gotten his draft notice and fled to Canada, she
guessed. She couldn't be sure, although the guy had talked about
it before taking off.

"I'm very sorry," he said.

They sat in silence for some moments until his voice broke it.
Someday, he said, someone would find her beautiful because of
what she had lost and what she had held onto.

She looked at him with cool disbelief. "My name is Nancy,"
she said.

"Harry Denman," he said.

She moved over beside him and ordered a second drink. He
asked how she had come to be here in Baltimore. "Tell me your
story."

Haltingly at first, hands on her glass and gently swirling it, she opened up. She had come up from Culpeper, Virginia, to work in a Congressional office. But the Congressman had been a lech, and she quit after two years, disillusioned. At one time she had considered majoring in art, so when a secretarial job came open at the Baltimore Museum of Art, she took it—putting her close every day to her beloved Picasso, Matisse, Cézanne.

Dangling her hair over her drink, she told how she had just gotten settled in the city when the boyfriend had vanished. Then, a month ago, her younger brother had gotten out of the Army and . . . he wasn't the same. He couldn't take care of himself. And her parents couldn't manage either, especially not her mother, who had rheumatoid arthritis. They all needed her at home, so she would probably have to give up her job, move back there, and care for everybody.

"Let me tell you about something a lot better than that drink you just ordered," Denman said. And with unconscious tact—grace, perhaps—he shared his own story and convictions. He spoke with understanding about her concerns for her brother and parents. Most of all he wanted her to know she was not alone.

"What I have, I give you," he said, "the name of Jesus Christ."

He took out an address book filled with names (there were so many—hundreds must have been crammed into the margins), asked her name and address, and promised to write her. Already she wanted to receive that letter.

"Pray for me," he said, and paid the bill, and went on his way.

Notes

1. Lynne Olson, "Dear Beatrice Fairfax . . . ," *American Heritage*, May–June 1992, 93.

2. Ibid.

3. Cardinal Henry Edward Manning, cited in "Pope Benedict XVI," *Christian Order*, June–July 2005.

4. Mark Twain, *The Innocents Abroad* (New York: Signet Classic, 1966), 27.

5. Ibid., 71–72.

6. Twain, *Autobiography of Mark Twain* (New York: Harper & Brothers, 1924), 2.

7. Jane Kenyon, *Otherwise* (St. Paul, MN: Graywolf Press, 1996), 214.

8. John Bayley, "Elegy for Iris," *New Yorker*, July 27, 1998, 45–46.

9. Ibid., 61.

10. Clifton Fadiman, ed., *The Little, Brown Book of Anecdotes* (Boston: Little, Brown, 1985), 323.

11. Ernest Fremont Tittle, "Footmen and Horses," in *A Mighty Fortress* (New York: Harper & Brothers, 1950), 19.

12. Barbara Brown Taylor, Interview by Bob Abernethy, *Religion & Ethics*, Public Broadcasting Service, December 1, 2000, episode no. 414.

13. Phillips Verner Bradford and Harvey Blume, *Ota Benga: The Pygmy in the Zoo* (New York: St. Martin's Press, 1992), 255.

14. Sue Halpern, *Four Wings and a Prayer* (New York: Vintage Books, 2001), 7–8.

15. Elizabeth Barrett Browning, *Aurora Leigh*, Book VII.

16. Pascal's amulet, translation by Patrick Denzil, *Pascal and Kierkegaard*, vol. 1 (Lutterworth Press, 1947), 76.

17. Max Picard, *The Flight from God* (Washington, D.C.: Regnery Gateway, 1951), 2.

Bibliography

This book grew out of three congregations and the stories of many parishioners and good friends. Before moving on to any other acknowledgments, I want to thank them for sharing these sacred stories.

ADVICE FOR LONELY HEARTS

Manning, Marie. *Ladies Then and Now.* New York: E.P. Dutton & Co., 1944.
Olson, Lynne. "Dear Beatrice Fairfax . . . ," *American Heritage*, (May–June 1992).
Thanks also to Manning Gasch, Marie Manning's grandson.

REMEMBER ME

Kaplan, Justin. *Mr. Clemens and Mark Twain.* New York: Simon & Schuster, 1966.
Thanks also to Norma Leary of the Jamestown (PA) Historical Society.
Twain, Mark. *The Innocents Abroad.* New York: Signet Classic, 1966.

A CONVERSATION

Bayley, John. "Elegy for Iris," *The New Yorker*, July 27, 1998.

HANDEL'S MESSIAH

Luckett, Richard. *Handel's Messiah: A Celebration.* San Diego: Harcourt Brace Jovanovich, 1992.

THE NEAREST STAR

Fadiman, Clifton, ed. *Little, Brown Book of Anecdotes.* Boston: Little, Brown & Co., 1985.

AND THEN IT HITS YOU

"Bulgarian President calls investigation into lightning-hit home." BBC News, May 16, 2003.

Edgar, Julie. "Boy hit by lightning: 'I'm lucky.'" *Detroit Free Press,* August 4, 2003.

"Lightning strikes twice for golfer." BBC News, May 16, 2003.

RUN THE RACE

Hampson, Rick. "Way out of the running: horse's 86 losses in a row could keep him off the track." *USA Today,* March 21, 2000.

Tittle, Ernest Fremont. *A Mighty Fortress.* New York: Harper & Brothers, 1950.

ULTIMA THULE

Ehrlich, Gretel. "Cold Comfort: Looking for the Sun in Greenland's Endless Night." *Harper's Magazine,* March 1997.

Tayler, Jeffrey. "This Side of Ultima Thule." *Atlantic Monthly,* April 1997.

TEETH SET ON EDGE

"Cannibal is not sick, says doctor." BBC News, December 29, 2003.

Harding, Luke. "Victim of cannibal agreed to be eaten." *The Guardian* (London), December 4, 2003.

"Sorry we roasted your relative, Fiji villagers say." *USA Today,* November 13, 2003.

SCOTTY'S CASTLE

Many thanks to the National Park Service.

SELLING THE EIFFEL TOWER

Johnson, James, and Miller, Floyd. *The Man Who Sold the Eiffel Tower.* Garden City, NY: Doubleday, 1961.

FIRSTHAND

Aebi, Tania. *Maiden Voyage.* New York: Ballantine Books, 1989.

THE VOICE OF ONE

Bradford, Phillips Verner, and Blume, Harvey. *Ota Benga: The Pygmy in the Zoo.* New York: St. Martin's Press, 1992.

Mitchell, Margaret. *Gone with the Wind.* New York: Macmillan Co., 1936.
Pyron, Darden Asbury. *Southern Daughter: the Life of Margaret Mitchell.* New York: Oxford University Press, 1991.

FIELD OF BLOOD

Flaubert, Gustave. *Three Tales.* West Drayton, Middlesex: Penguin Books, 1961.
Tabor, James D. *The Jesus Dynasty.* New York: Simon & Schuster, 2006.

SEARCHING AND KNOWING

Throughout July of 2003, the Fremont (Michigan) *Times-Indicator* carried news accounts of this case.

BRIDE OF CHRIST

Willimon, William. "Cleaning Up the Wedding." *The Christian Century,* June 6, 1979.

THE SECOND COMING

Smith, Asbury, and Potts, J. Manning. *Love Abounds: A Profile of Harry Denman, a Modern Disciple.* Nashville: The Upper Room, 1965.